LEARN
TO PLAY
UKULELE

LEARN
TO PLAY
UKULELE

PHIL CAPONE

CHARTWELL
BOOKS, INC.

A QUARTO BOOK

Published in 2012 by
Chartwell Books, Inc.
A division of Book Sales, Inc.
276 Fifth Avenue, Suite 206
New York, New York 10001
USA

ISBN-13: 978-0-7858-2904-1
QUAR.LPU

Conceived, designed, and produced by
Quarto Publishing plc
The Old Brewery,
6 Blundell Street
London N7 9BH

Project editor: Chloe Todd Fordham
Art editor: Jacqueline Palmer
Designer: Anna Formanek
Photographer: Martin Norris

Art director: Caroline Guest
Creative director: Moira Clinch
Publisher: Paul Carslake

Color separation in Hong Kong by
Modern Age Repro House Limited
Printed in China by
Midas Printing International Limited

10 9 8 7 6 5 4 3 2 1

Contents

Introduction

The ukulele, or "uke," as it's commonly referred to, has enjoyed a renaissance in recent years. Sales of this incredibly popular instrument continue to soar, thanks primarily to the Internet and sites like YouTube, where access to the inspirational performances of virtuoso players like Jake Shimabukuro or talented singer-songwriters such as Julia Nunes is quick and easy.

The ukulele's history can be traced back to Hawaii in the late 19th century when Portuguese immigrants introduced the instrument to the idyllic Pacific island. The Hawaiian word *ukulele* roughly translates as "jumping flea," presumably something to do with the instrument's diminutive proportions. The instrument arrived in the USA during the early 20th century, and from there its appeal quickly spread across the globe. Popularity peaked during the instrument's heyday in the 1950s and early 1960s, with interest declining rapidly throughout the 1970s and 1980s. By the 1990s sales had reached such an all-time low that many manufacturers (including the famous guitar makers C.F. Martin & Co) ceased production of the instrument. One of the pivotal moments in the uke's resurgence in popularity was Paul McCartney's 2002 tribute concert for his former Beatles bandmate George Harrison, who had died the previous year. Harrison was well known for his love of the ukulele (he apparently kept several in the boot of his car because "you never know when you might need a ukulele"), but it was McCartney's ukulele performances on that day that undoubtedly rekindled the public's interest.

For many devotees of course, the uke has never been out of fashion, and it's easy to see why; cheap to buy, extremely portable, and easier to play than a guitar. However, most people who buy a uke never get further than strumming a few simple chord shapes, so they soon get bored, leaving the uke to gather dust in the attic. So how can you prevent this from happening? Guitar students have an almost endless resource of teaching material at their disposal. But if you want to do more than learn a few basic chord shapes on the uke, finding the right teach-yourself manual that will inspire you and allow you to progress at your own pace is not so easy. That's where this handy and informative tutorial comes in.

There are 20 lessons in this book, plus an extensive reference section that includes useful scale patterns in every key. The lessons start with the basics (tuning, how to hold the uke, hand positions, etc.), then build your technique gradually using clear, easy-to-understand step-by-step illustrations that make learning each new skill easy and fun. The inclusion of both conventional and TAB notation helps to make your progress effortless and frustration-free, even if you can't read music. An accompanying CD also lets you hear exactly how each piece should sound once completed.

Finally, the handy and compact form makes this book extremely portable (just like the uke!) so you can take it with you wherever you go. The spiral binding means you can open it out flat, so it's a pleasure to use and guaranteed to make your practice sessions productive. So grab your uke and let's get started.

Sir Paul McCartney rekindled our love for the ukulele during his tribute "Concert for George" at the Royal Albert Hall, London in 2002. Here, Sir Paul is playing a left-handed model.

About This Book

This book is designed to help you learn to play the ukulele, from buying your first uke to practicing scales and learning songs.

Lessons (pages 14–111)

20 carefully structured lessons take you step by step through the essentials of learning to play the ukulele.

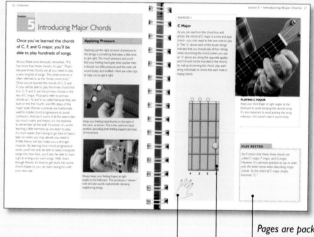

Pages are packed full of useful tips to ensure you play to your full potential.

Graphic chord boxes show you exactly where to place your fingers on the neck of the ukulele.

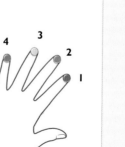

This hand icon describes your fretting hand. When you see a red dot on a chord box, use your index finger; when you see a blue dot, use your middle finger; yellow denotes your ring finger; and green your pinky. Easy! The icon features throughout the book as a reminder, but you will soon find you can do without it.

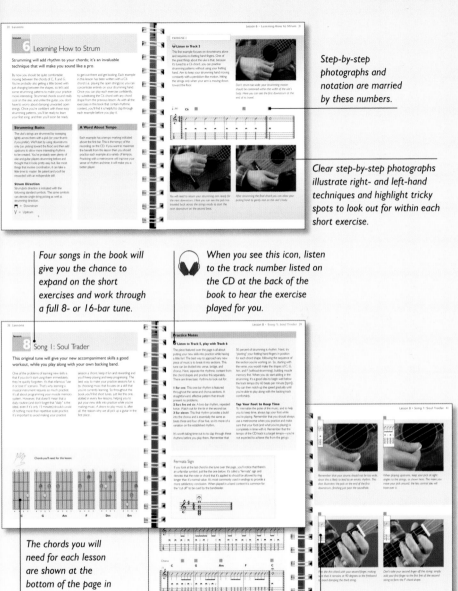

Step-by-step photographs and notation are married by these numbers.

Clear step-by-step photographs illustrate right- and left-hand techniques and highlight tricky spots to look out for within each short exercise.

Four songs in the book will give you the chance to expand on the short exercises and work through a full 8- or 16-bar tune.

When you see this icon, listen to the track number listed on the CD at the back of the book to hear the exercise played for you.

The chords you will need for each lesson are shown at the bottom of the page in neat diagrams.

Fragments of the musical notation are placed by the photographs so that you can easily locate the right part of the music for each step.

Pentatonic Scale Library
(pages 112–149)

A scale library covers major and minor pentatonic scales; an essential resource for the uke player. See page 112 for a guide to the information that is included on the diagrams.

Each chord in the pentatonic scale library is spelled out from its root note with the intervals marked.

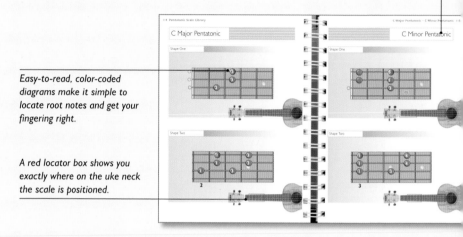

Easy-to-read, color-coded diagrams make it simple to locate root notes and get your fingering right.

A red locator box shows you exactly where on the uke neck the scale is positioned.

Chord Library (pages 150–187)

A useful library of sixth, seventh, ninth, and diminished chords follows to help you expand your chord vocabulary. See page 150 for a guide to the information that is included on the diagrams.

Chords are arranged by root chord which is spelled out in the top corners.

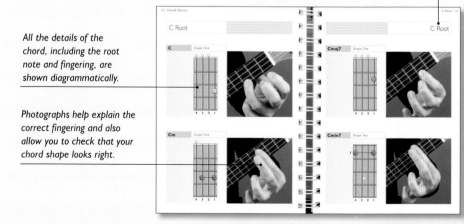

All the details of the chord, including the root note and fingering, are shown diagrammatically.

Photographs help explain the correct fingering and also allow you to check that your chord shape looks right.

Jake Shimabukuro found fame on YouTube with his stunning performance of "While My Guitar Gently Weeps." His jaw-dropping virtuosity and complex arrangements have secured him a huge fanbase.

Instant Note Finder

In order to get the most out of your playing, you must at some stage engage with learning what the notes on each string are. While this may seem a daunting task to start with, there is some good news. The progression of notes both up and down the neck is a fixed and repeating sequence of 12 notes.

The crucial things to know are the notes of the open strings—these should already be familiar from tuning up—and the names of the notes at a couple of landmark frets on all four strings. The rest is then filling in the gaps.

The diagram here is a map showing the name of the note on any given fret on all four strings. This information is vital when we come to deal with movable chords.

Western music has (as a norm) 12 given steps or pitches between any note and the same note an octave higher or lower.

Getting Started

To get started, let's look at an open string, the third string, whose open note is C, and the notes we encounter on the way to hitting the note of C again one octave higher.

The ukulele, like most fretted instruments, has 12 frets between the open string and the octave of that note, allowing 12 notes to be played between the open string and the same note one octave higher. We can see that the names of the notes at the twelfth fret are the same as the names of the open strings.

Without worrying what the names of the notes are yet, play any open string, then, using your first finger to hold down the notes, play the string at the first fret, then the second, and so on all the way to the twelfth fret. You have musically speaking just covered the distance of one octave. If we travel beyond the twelfth fret—into the "dusty end"—we see that the sequence repeats, the thirteenth fret being the same note as the first fret.

Now, play the open string again, then play that string at the twelfth fret. Your ears will tell you that the fretted note is "higher" than the open string—but, hopefully, you will hear they are somehow the same. They are both the same note one octave apart.

the twelfth fret, let's go back and plot our way along the 12 fret journey. This will give us the whole chromatic picture of the fretboard landscape.

Look at the picture, choose a string, and say the name of each note in turn. Irrespective of which string you've chosen, you will soon encounter a fret that appears to have two notes with different names/symbols there. This may seem confusing at first, but is something of a glass half full or empty phenomenon. To give it its proper name: enharmonic equivalents. Simply two names for the same thing. The same pitch—two possible ways of naming it. C♯ (C sharp) is the same sound/pitch as D♭ (D flat) in this instance. C♯, also known as D♭, is the intermediate note between C and D.

Another possible option for a dual named note is B♭, which could also be called A♯, but in practice A♯ is hardly (if ever) used as a name for that note. If you repeat the same exercise on a different string, although you start at a different note, it will become apparent that the sequence is the same as the string you used at first, that is to say, wherever you start on the 12-note sequence, the order of the notes is the same: C always follows B and precedes C♯, and so on.

Nut

Third Fret

Fifth Fret

Seventh Fret

Tenth Fret

Twelfth Fret

Notes of the open strings

Octave
Sequence starts again from here—as if from open strings.

PLAY BETTER

Getting to know all the notes on all the strings is a good aspiration. Start by learning the notes between the open strings and the fifth fret. Adding the notes up to the seventh fret would be the next logical step, and from there up to the twelfth. Ultimately, aim to be able to name/find any note on any string without having to count along from the open string.

Lessons

Notation Guide

Open position (first fret) chord box:

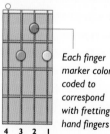

Each finger marker color coded to correspond with fretting hand fingers

4 3 2 1

String numbers clearly labeled

This hand icon describes your fretting hand. When you see a red dot on a chord box, use your index finger; when you see a blue dot, use your middle finger; yellow denotes your ring finger; and green your pinky.

Chord box beginning on second fret:

2

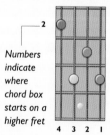

Numbers indicate where chord box starts on a higher fret

4 3 2 1

KEY

O = open string included in chord

●━● = barre or semibarre (color coded to indicate finger used)

DIRECTIONAL SYMBOLS

You will see directional symbols just above the TAB stave. A square symbol indicates down-picks and an arrow indicates up-picks. The same symbols denote downstrums and upstrums.

  down-pick or downstrum

V up-pick or upstrum

This is the section of the book where you will learn all of the skills you'll need to become a proficient ukulele player. The lessons are progressive and designed to build your technique while you're playing. By the time you've completed all the lessons in this book, you'll know all of the essential tips and tricks that will enable you to play the uke.

To get the most out of this book, you should aim to review the previous lessons as often as you can, preferably at the start of every practice session. This will reinforce your knowledge and boost your confidence.

STRUMMING HAND FINGER SYMBOLS

Abbreviations of the traditional Spanish names are used throughout for the fingers of your strumming hand; using numbers would create confusion with the fretting hand.

p (*pulgar*) = thumb
i (*indice*) = index
m (*medio*) = middle
a (*anillo*) = ring

1 Sizes and Tunings

If you haven't bought your "uke" yet, this chapter will help you to decide which type is right for you.

The four main sizes of ukulele are: soprano, concert, tenor, and baritone. The soprano, concert, and tenor are all tuned to what is known as C6 tuning. When the open strings are strummed they make the sound of a C6 chord. Unlike the guitar, the strings do not ascend in pitch sequence. The fourth string (lowest) is tuned an octave higher so that it is actually a perfect fifth higher than the third string. This type of tuning is called reentrant tuning and is also found on other stringed instruments such as the banjo, sitar, and lute. The soprano ukulele was originally tuned to D6 chord a tone (two frets) higher, but it is now also commonly tuned to C6. The only uke that is tuned differently is the baritone, which is generally tuned the same as the top four strings of the guitar, so it sounds lower than the other three sizes. For the purposes of this book, we will be using the standard C6 tuning throughout. This really rules out the more specialized baritone uke, so your choice then depends entirely on which size suits your fingers best. Let's take an in-depth look at the three most popular sizes:

Soprano

The soprano is the smallest of the four uke sizes. It is sometimes referred to as "standard" because it is the same size as the original Hawaiian ukuleles that became very popular throughout the USA and Europe in the early 20th century. The soprano's dimensions are diminutive to say the least; it's overall length being just 21 in (53 cm). Although this sounds nice and compact, you have to remember that with a scale length (that's the distance between the nut and the bridge) of just 13 in (33 cm) the frets are going to be very close together indeed. That makes this size the ideal junior choice; but adults may find it rather cramped when fretting notes, particularly higher up the neck.

UKE FACT FILE

Body size: Soprano
Standard tuning: G4/C4/E4/A4
Scale length: 13 in (33 cm)
Overall length: 21 in (53 cm)

Concert

The concert ukulele arrived back in the 1920s when it was developed to improve the volume and tone of the diminutive soprano. Both the length and scale length of this instrument are 2 in (5.1 cm) greater than the soprano, making this instrument more playable. The larger body size also gives this uke a warmer, less shrill tone than the soprano. This instrument is an ideal choice if you would like a little more space on the fretboard, but want to remain close to the compact dimensions of the original uke. This is the ideal uke choice for adults with smallish hands.

UKE FACT FILE

Body size: Concert
Standard tuning: G4/C4/E4/A4
Scale length: 15 in (38 cm)
Overall length: 23 in (58 cm)

Tenor

The tenor uke followed hot on the heels of the concert model; it also first appeared during the 1920s. This instrument not only provided greater volume levels, but also an increased bass presence on low notes. With a scale length that is 4 in (10.2 cm) longer than the soprano ukulele, this model is the ideal choice for male students, those with larger hands, or simply to provide more accessibility to the higher frets, for those wishing to do more than just strum a few chords. However, as with most things in life, there is a trade off! It's worth remembering that, as the scale length increases, string tension also increases. This results in slightly more pressure being required to fret notes on a tenor than the equivalent notes on a concert or soprano. However, this difference is pretty slight; if you already play guitar, you'll find the tenor uke is easy to play.

UKE FACT FILE

Body size: Tenor
Standard tuning: G4/C4/E4/A4
Scale length: 17 in (43 cm)
Overall length: 26 in (66 cm)

2 Are You Sitting Comfortably?

Time spent improving your posture, whether you're sitting or standing, is time well spent.

Bad posture can cause muscular problems; it can make practicing a chore because you won't feel relaxed. It is really important to feel comfortable when you're practicing. It should be an enjoyable experience where the music takes you to another place, far from the stresses of modern life. Practicing can be as deeply rewarding as meditation, but only if you're not suffering from aches and pains caused by bad posture. Most players practice sitting down simply because it's more comfortable; it allows them to focus on refining their technique. Although the default learning position for any stringed instrument is sitting, we'll also cover the essential points to remember when standing with your uke too.

The fretting hand should cradle the neck of the ukulele so that the uke is more or less at a 45-degree angle to the floor.

The ukulele should be snug against the player's body and angled slightly back, making it possible to see the fingers of the fretting hand.

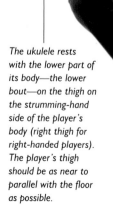

Sitting

Playing sitting down is the favored default position, and certainly may be the easier option in the early stages of learning to play. The ideal piece of furniture will be a stool or firm, arm-less chair. The optimum height of this will vary from player to player, but your aim is to sit with a straight back and both feet on the floor. Try to avoid slouching and "wrapping" yourself over the uke: this will be more tiring in the long run, and certainly have an adverse effect on your breathing if you are also singing.

The ukulele rests with the lower part of its body—the lower bout—on the thigh on the strumming-hand side of the player's body (right thigh for right-handed players). The player's thigh should be as near to parallel with the floor as possible.

Standing

To play the ukulele standing up, it is conventional not to use a strap to support the instrument, as a guitarist or banjo player would. We are therefore faced with the dual task of holding and playing the ukulele at the same time. Don't get too hung up on the geometry and angles here. They are rule-of-thumb suggestions; no set squares or spirit levels are required!

Grip the top side of the uke's lower body under the forearm of the strumming arm.

The fretting hand cradles the neck in the crook between the first finger and thumb, giving just enough lift to maintain a viable playing position, with the headstock higher than the body— something around 30 degrees from horizontal should feel comfortable.

PLAY BETTER

You may be tempted to skip this chapter, but getting your posture right is very important. An awkward playing position makes practicing hard work, meaning you'll spend less time with your instrument. So learning how to hold your uke correctly will, without question, make you a better player.

lesson

3 Tuning Your Uke

An out of tune ukulele is bad news because it will make you sound terrible. Find out how to tune perfectly in this essential lesson.

It's only natural that you'll want to start playing your uke straight away, but don't be tempted to skip this lesson. Learning how to tune your instrument (and checking the tuning every time you pick it up) will ensure that you'll only ever need to make minor adjustments; this is much easier than trying to tune up an instrument that's way out of tune. Don't forget, too, that an out of tune instrument will make you sound bad, so no matter how hard you've practiced, your

friends will not be impressed with the results. Because the uke is tuned to a chord, you'll soon find that it's easy to tell when something's not quite right. Brush your pick, fingers, or thumb slowly across the strings and you should hear a sweet sounding C6 chord. If you don't, then you need to check your tuning. You can use any or all of the following methods to get your uke back in tune and sounding sweet again.

Second and third strings (E):	First and second strings (A):	Fourth and first strings (A):

```
T   0                    0                    0
A        4                    5
B                                       2
```

Only one string at a time should be sounded for an accurate reading when using a tuner. Here, you can see the pick in position ready to play the third string.

Turn the machine head slowly as you play the string. You'll probably only need to move it a fraction of a turn to get it in tune.

Tuning by Ear

This method is called "relative tuning" since it will only verify that the uke is in tune with itself. The TAB opposite shows you how you can check the three pairs of strings and make sure they're nicely in tune with each other. When fretted as indicated in the TAB, each pair of strings will produce the same note. Play the strings simultaneously for best results. When the strings are nearly in tune, you will hear a beating or pulsating effect caused by the slight difference in pitch. As the pitches get closer the beating slows, disappearing altogether once the strings are in tune. It's easier to start by tuning the fretted third string against the open second string, but you can tune the strings in any order. Obviously the main drawback of this method is that if you start on an out of tune string, you'll actually end up detuning all the strings. It's best to check each pair of strings first and decide which ones are out of tune before you start making any adjustments.

Using a Tuner

An electronic tuner will keep your uke in concert pitch, so it's definitely worth investing in one. You can buy specialist ukulele tuners, but most modern guitar tuners will work just as well. The "clip on" tuners are the best ones to get. These clamp onto the uke's headstock and automatically detect which string you're playing by picking up string vibrations. When you play an open string, the tuner will indicate whether it is flat, sharp, or in tune, usually via arrows on an LCD display. Then all you have to do is adjust the appropriate tuning head. If your uke is a long way out of tune, an electric tuner may not be able to identify the string pitches correctly. If this happens, don't be afraid to ask your local music store (or a uke-playing friend!) for help. Don't forget that you can also use the tuning notes provided on the accompanying CD.

◖ Listen to Track I

To help you get in tune, we've included some tuning notes on the accompanying CD—each string is played three times before moving to the next, starting with the first (high A) string.

PLAY BETTER

Learning to tune quickly and efficiently will make you a better musician. You can then spend less time tuning and more time playing. The music you create will also sound much sweeter! If you're using an electronic tuner with a built-in mic, rest the tuner on your leg, as close to the uke as possible.

4 Reading Notation

Don't worry if you can't read music, reading TAB is easy. This lesson shows you how.

Every example in this book has been annotated using a combination of conventional notation (what musicians call "the dots") and TAB (short for tablature). The majority of music publishers today use this system, so you're probably already used to seeing it. If you're not, don't worry; this lesson will explain everything you need to know! While it's not necessary to be able to read conventional notation to get the most from this book, you'll find a little time spent now on understanding the basics will be well worth it. Conventional notation is extremely useful in two essential areas: 1) for describing rhythmic content; and 2) adding fretting hand fingering detail (this is not possible when using TAB alone).

Reading Notes

EXERCISE 1

The traditional five-line stave can be used for any instrument that reads from the treble clef. Some instruments read from different clefs; these change the range of notes the stave can display. Each line and space of the treble clef has a corresponding letter name that represents a musical note, as shown in the example below.

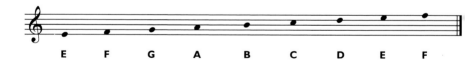

E	F	G	A	B	C	D	E	F

EXERCISE 2

In this example, you can see how the four lines of the TAB stave represent the
four strings of the uke. To read TAB all you have to do is convert the number
on the line to a fret on the corresponding string.

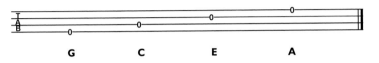

G   C   E   A

EXERCISE 3

It's really very easy to read notes when using this system. Below is the scale of
C major, which can easily be transferred to the uke without looking at the top stave
at all. That's because the notes in the conventional stave don't contain any additional
information; they've been written as solid note heads that describe pitch only. That
all-important rhythmic content will be added in the next exercise, over the page.

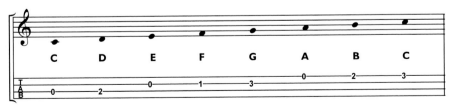

C   D   E   F   G   A   B   C

Reading Rhythms

Here, you can see how the notes written in conventional notation describe position and duration (i.e. rhythm) as well as pitch. Although these symbols may look a little strange, with a little practice you'll soon be able to read rhythms at sight. Remember that where the note is placed on the stave describes the pitch. So what pitch would all these notes be?

For each of the notes above, there's an equivalent rest—as you can see below. That's because the gaps between notes are just as important as the notes themselves; it's a mixture of these two elements that creates rhythm.

EXERCISE 6

In this example, a simple three-note riff is demonstrated using a combination of TAB and conventional notation. By looking at the top stave, we can see that the first two notes are quarter notes that ring for one beat each; the last note is a half note and rings for two beats. The "1" added beside the second note indicates that this is a fretted note and should be played using your first finger. Look at the TAB below and it's easy to see which strings the notes are played on. Remember that a "0" indicates an open string.

EXERCISE 7

Strumming rhythms are generally written using the conventional stave alone. To keep things nice and simple, slash note heads are used, so there are no pitches to worry about. When used in conjunction with a chord symbol, this is all the information you'll need to start playing cool grooves. Slash rhythms are so-called because a diagonal line replaces the regular note head. We'll be looking at strumming rhythms in more detail in Lesson Six (page 30).

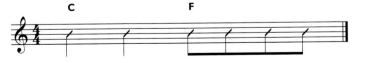

5 Introducing Major Chords

Once you've learned the chords of C, F, and G major, you'll be able to play hundreds of songs.

As Lou Reed once famously remarked, "If it has more than three chords, it's jazz." That's because three chords are all you need to play a very long list of songs. This phenomenon is often referred to as the "three chord trick." Once you've learned the chords of C, F, and G you will be able to play the three chord trick too. C, F, and G are the primary chords in the key of C major. Musicians refer to primary chords as I, IV, and V, so-called because they are built on the first, fourth, and fifth steps of the major scale (Roman numerals are traditionally used to notate chord progressions to avoid confusion). And don't worry if all this seems like too much maths and theory, it's not essential to remember all this stuff. However, it's worth learning a little harmony as you learn to play; it's much easier than having to go back to basics later on when you may decide you need it. A little theory will also make you a stronger musician. By learning how chord progressions work, you'll not only be able to easily transpose songs into new keys, you'll also be able to have a go at writing your own songs. Well, that's enough theory; it's time to get stuck into some chord shapes so you can start having fun with your new uke.

Applying Pressure

Applying just the right amount of pressure to the strings is something that takes a little time to get right. Too much pressure and you'll find your fretting hand gets tired quicker than it should; too little pressure and the note will sound buzzy and muffled. Here are a few tips to help you to get it right.

Keep your fretting hand thumb on the back of the neck, as shown. This is the optimum hand position, providing both fretting support and ease of movement.

Always keep your fretting fingers at right angles to the fretboard. This produces a "cleaner" note and also avoids inadvertently damping neighboring strings.

EXERCISE I

C Major

As you can see from the chord box and photo, the chord of C major is a nice and easy chord—you only need to fret one note to play it. The "o" above each of the lower strings indicates that you should play all four strings when strumming this chord (when you see an "x" above any string the opposite applies and it should not be included in the chord). As well as strumming the chord, play each string individually to check that each note is ringing clearly.

PLAYING C MAJOR

Keep your third finger at right angles to the fretboard to avoid damping the second string. It's also important to avoid pushing the string sideways—this would make it sound sharp.

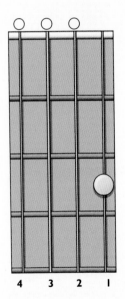

PLAY BETTER

You'll notice that these three chords are called C major, F major, and G major. However, it's common practice to say or write only the letter name when describing major chords. So the chord of C major simply becomes "C."

EXERCISE 2

F Major

The chord of F major consists of two fretted notes, so it's slightly trickier to play than a C chord. Keeping your thumb in position on the back of the neck (as illustrated in Applying Pressure at the start of this lesson) will enable you to fret the notes more easily and avoid damping the open first and third strings (indicated by the "o" above them). It's a good idea to just practice "planting" your fingers in the right place by lifting them on and off the strings. You can do this without strumming the chord.

PLAYING F MAJOR

Because there are open strings each side of the fretted notes, it's very important to ensure that you're fingers fret the notes nice and cleanly to avoid muting them.

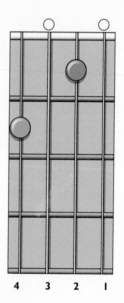

4   3   2   1

Famous Three Chord Songs

Here's a short list of some classic songs that can be played with the three chord trick. (Note: some of these songs were originally recorded in other keys.)

Blue Suede Shoes—Elvis Presley
Johnny B Goode—Chuck Berry
Bye Bye Love—The Everly Brothers
Wild Thing—The Troggs/Jimi Hendrix
Peaceful Easy Feeling—The Eagles
Sweet Home Alabama—Lynyrd Skynyrd
Rock & Roll—Led Zeppelin
Love Me Do—The Beatles
La Bamba—Richie Valens
Lay Down Sally—Eric Clapton
Big Yellow Taxi—Joni Mitchell
Blowin' In The Wind—Bob Dylan

EXERCISE 3

G Major

The final chord in this lesson is G major. This chord involves fretting three strings simultaneously, so it's harder to play than both C and F. However, it's still quite an easy chord shape once you've trained your fingers to move to the right frets (practice "planting" your fingers in the right place by simply lifting them on and off the strings). For the guitarists among you, this shape will be instantly recognized as a D chord shape. However, because of the different tuning used on the uke it produces a G chord and not D, as it would on the guitar.

PLAYING G MAJOR

It's the second string that can cause problems in this chord; it needs to be fretted cleanly with the third finger to avoid touching the neighboring strings. Keep all of your fingers angled nicely, as shown here.

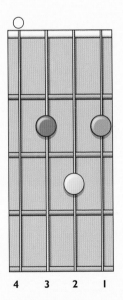

4   3   2   I

6 Learning How to Strum

Strumming will add rhythm to your chords; it's an invaluable technique that will make you sound like a pro.

By now you should be quite comfortable moving between the chords of C, F, and G. You're probably also getting a little bored with just changing between the shapes, so let's add some strumming patterns to make your practice more interesting. Strummed chords sound really cool on the uke, and unlike the guitar, you don't have to worry about damping unwanted open strings. Once you're confident with these easy strumming patterns, you'll be ready to learn your first song, and then you'll soon be ready to get out there and get busking. Each example in this lesson has been written with a C6 chord (i.e. playing the open strings) so you can concentrate entirely on your strumming hand. Once you can play each exercise confidently, try substituting the C6 chord with any chord shape from the previous lesson. As with all the exercises in this book that contain rhythmic content, you'll find it is helpful to clap through each example before you play it.

Strumming Basics

The uke's strings are strummed by sweeping lightly across them with a pick (or your thumb if you prefer). We'll start by using downstrums only (i.e. picking toward the floor) and then add upstrums to allow more interesting rhythms to be created. You've probably seen plenty of uke and guitar players strumming before and thought that it looks pretty easy but, like most things that involve coordination, it can take a little time to master. Be patient and you'll be rewarded with an indispensible skill.

Strum Direction

Strum/pick direction is indicated with the following standard symbols. The same symbols can denote single string picking as well as strumming direction.

⊓ = Downstrum

V = Upstrum

A Word About Tempo

Each example has a tempo marking indicated above the first bar. This is the tempo of the recording on the CD. If you want to maximize the benefit from this lesson then you should practice each example at a variety of tempos. Practicing with a metronome will improve your sense of rhythm and time; it will make you a better player.

EXERCISE I

🕪 Listen to Track 2

This first example focuses on downstrums alone and requires no fretting hand fingers. One of the great things about the uke is that, because it's tuned to a C6 chord, you can practice strumming patterns without using your fretting hand. Aim to keep your strumming hand moving constantly with a pendulum-like motion, hitting the strings only when your arm is moving down toward the floor.

Don't strum too wide; your strumming motion should be contained within the width of the uke's body. Here you can see the first downstrum at the end of its travel.

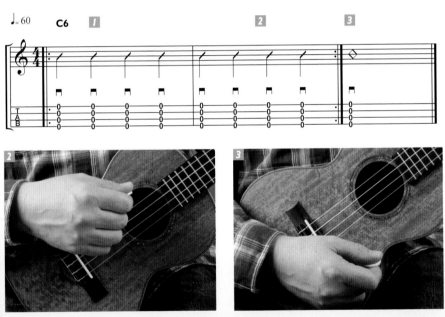

You will need to return your strumming arm ready for the next downstrum. Here you can see the pick has traveled back across the strings ready to start the next downstrum on the second beat.

After strumming the final chord you can allow your picking hand to gently rest on the uke's body.

EXERCISE 2

🎧 **Listen to Track 3**

In the first example, you played a downstrum on every beat. But in order to do this, your strumming arm had to return to its original position ready for the next downstrum; in effect you were playing silent upstrums. In this next example we're going to sound those upstrums by allowing the pick to make contact with the strings. Notice that you'll only play upstrums in the second bar as indicated by the picking symbols above the TAB.

Counting the Beats

The second bars of Exercise Two and Exercise Three contain only eighth notes (i.e. each beat is divided into two notes). To make it easier to play eighth notes correctly you can add an "+" between the beats when counting. So instead of counting 1, 2, 3, 4, count 1 +, 2 +, 3 +, 4 +. Remember to always clap rhythms before you play them for best results.

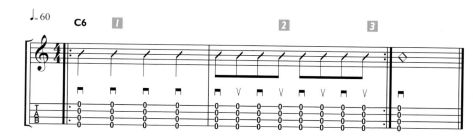

After playing the first chord in bar one, your strumming arm moves back across the strings, effectively playing a silent upstrum.

At exactly the same point in the second bar, the pick makes contact with the strings to play the first upstrum on the offbeat of beat one.

Check to make sure that the endpoint of your upstrum does not travel outside of the uke's body. Ideally, the upstrum should travel just past the edge of the soundhole, as shown.

🎧 Listen to Track 4

This example incorporates syncopation by using a silent downstrum. Syncopation is created when weak beats are accented or strong beats are omitted. In this example, syncopation occurs in the second bar where a tie is used to join two eighth notes together, so nothing sounds on the third beat. Although it feels very natural to play silent upstrums—you can do this without thinking about it—it's very different playing silent downstrums. That's because they fall on the "strong" beats, so you instinctively want to play them. Take your time and remember to keep that strumming arm moving constantly and evenly.

The downstrums in the first bar should travel no farther than the width of the uke's body. Here, we show the strumming arm having just played the first chord on beat one.

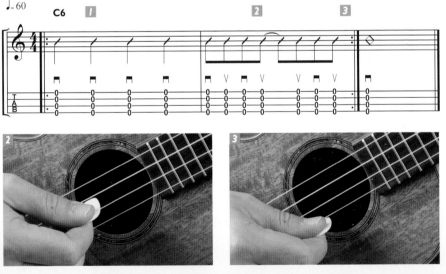

On the third beat of the second bar, although the strings are not sounded, your strumming arm should still play a silent downstrum with the pick lifted off the strings, as shown.

After playing the silent downstrum, the strumming arm moves upward with the pick, now making contact with the strings again.

7 Introducing Minor Chords

The three-chord trick is just that: a trick. In this lesson, we'll be learning the three indispensible minor chords: Am, Dm, and Em.

It's all very well being able to play hundreds of songs with just three chords, but the downside is that you won't be able to play the many more hundreds of songs that contain minor chords. Minor chords are the opposite of the bright, happy sounding major chords; they sound melancholic and sad. But that doesn't mean you can only play sad songs with minor chords; they provide contrast and harmonic interest when mixed with major chords. So you'll generally find that most songs, even those written in major keys, also contain minor chords. They also sound great on a uke; there's something about the higher register of the uke that makes minor chords sound sweeter, even a touch optimistic.

Fretting with Three Fingers

So far we've only learned one chord that requires the use of three fretting hand fingers simultaneously; that was the chord of G major. Remember, that was the shape that resembled a D chord on guitar. In this lesson, both Dm and Em require the use of three fretting hand fingers, so they will take a little more time to master.

The advice given for fretting hand position in Lesson Five is just as important in this lesson. So remember to always keep your thumb in position at the back of the neck; this offers support while still allowing the fingers to move freely. It's also important to make sure that you always fret notes with your fingers at 90 degrees to the fretboard. This avoids inadvertently damping any neighboring strings, ensuring that all four notes of the chord shape can be heard. Remember that you should also pick each string individually when learning new shapes to double check this.

PLAY BETTER

The best way to memorize new chord shapes is to play them in short bursts as often as you can. Don't sit and practice chord shapes for hours on end; instead keep your uke handy so that when you've got five minutes to spare you can quickly recap all your new shapes.

A Minor

The first minor chord of the lesson is a nice and easy chord to play, since it only requires the use of your second finger. Don't forget too that an "o" above a string indicates that it should be included when playing the chord. To make sure that you're fretting the fourth string nice and cleanly (and not touching the third string), play each string individually as well as strumming the strings simultaneously. This helps to check that each is ringing clearly and cleanly.

PLAYING Am

Keep your second finger at right angles to the fretboard to avoid damping the third string. Notice that the thumb is also securely placed behind the neck, supporting the fingers while allowing them to move freely.

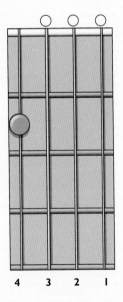

4   3   2   I

D Minor

The chord of D minor is played with your first, second, and third fretting hand fingers. Remember to keep your thumb in position on the back of the neck to allow your fingers to fret the notes easily. This also makes it much easier to keep your fingers at 90 degrees to the fretboard to avoid inadvertently damping the neighboring strings. Don't forget that it's also good to practice "planting" your fingers in position. Simply lift them on and off the strings without strumming the chord a few times to build muscle memory.

PLAYING Dm

Always keep your uke in an upright position, as demonstrated here. Holding the uke at an angle will compromise your fretting hand position, making it difficult to fret chords accurately and cleanly.

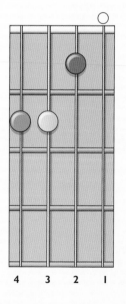

4   3   2   1

PLAY BETTER

Just as with the major chords in Lesson Five, these three chords are given their full titles of C minor, F minor, and G minor. Although you would say the full name when describing them verbally, it is sufficient just to write "min" or even "m" when notating them.

EXERCISE 3

E Minor

The final chord for this lesson is E minor. Just like the previous chord, this chord also involves fretting three strings simultaneously. As always, take your time when learning new shapes and follow the golden rules of correct fretting hand thumb and finger positioning, as previously outlined. Once again, the guitarists out there will recognize this shape, since it resembles the chord of Am on guitar. However, because the uke is tuned to an open C6 chord, it will produce an Em chord and not Am as it would when played on guitar.

PLAYING Em

When fretting notes on adjacent frets, it's important to spread your fingers evenly. This will allow you to place your fingers snugly behind each fret and to produce louder, clearer notes.

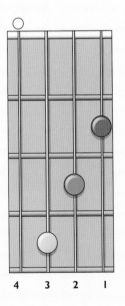

4   3   2   I

lesson

8 Song 1: Soul Trader

This original tune will give your new accompaniment skills a good workout, while you play along with your own backing band.

One of the problems of learning new skills is that if you don't start using them immediately, they're quickly forgotten. It's that infamous "use it or lose it" scenario. That's why learning a musical instrument requires so much practice; it's all about programming your muscle memory system. However, that doesn't mean that a daily routine (and don't forget that "daily" is the ideal, even if it's only 15 minutes) should consist of nothing more than repetitive scale practice. It's important to avoid making your practice

session a chore; keep it fun and rewarding and you'll keep playing and keep progressing. The best way to make your practice sessions fun is by choosing music that focuses on a skill that you're currently learning. So throughout this book you'll find short tunes, just like this one, slotted in every few lessons, helping you to put your new skills into practice while you're making music. A desire to play music is, after all, the reason why we all pick up a ukulele in the first place.

Chords you'll need for this lesson:

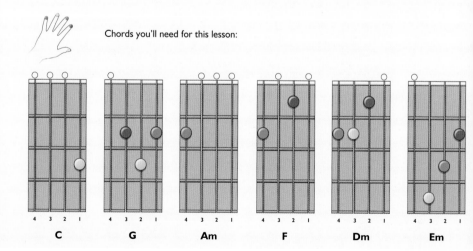

Practice Notes

🎧 **Listen to Track 5, play with Track 6**

The piece featured over the page is all about putting your new skills into practice while having a little fun! The best way to approach any new piece of music is to break it into sections. This tune can be divided into verse, bridge, and chorus. Next, separate the rhythmic content from the chord shapes and practice this separately. There are three basic rhythms to look out for:

1 Bar one: This one-bar rhythm is featured throughout the verse and chorus sections. A straightforward, effective pattern that should present no problems.

2 Bars five and six: A two-bar rhythm, repeated twice. Watch out for the tie in the second bar.

3 Bar eleven: This final rhythm provides a build into the chorus and is essentially the same as beats three and four of bar five, so it's more of a variation on the established rhythm.

It's worth taking time out to clap through these rhythms before you play them. Remember that

50 percent of strumming is rhythm. Next, try "planting" your fretting hand fingers in position for each chord shape, following the sequence of the section you're working on. So, starting with the verse, you would make the shapes of C, G, Am, and F (without strumming), building muscle memory first. When you do start adding in the strumming, it's a good idea to begin well below the track tempo (try 60 beats per minute [bpm]). You can then notch up the speed gradually until you're able to play along with the backing track comfortably.

Tap Your Foot to Keep Time

To internalize the pulse of the music, and to help you to keep time, always tap your foot while you're playing. Remember that you should always use a metronome when you practice and make sure that your foot (and what you're playing) is completely in time with it. Remember that the tempo of the CD track is a target tempo—you're not expected to achieve this from the get-go.

Fermata Sign

If you look at the last chord in the tune over the page, you'll notice that there's an unfamiliar symbol, just like the one below. It's called a "fermata" sign and denotes that the note or chord that it's applied to should be allowed to ring longer than it's normal value. It's most commonly used in endings to provide a more satisfactory conclusion. When played in a band context it is common for the "cut off" to be cued by the bandleader.

Soul Trader

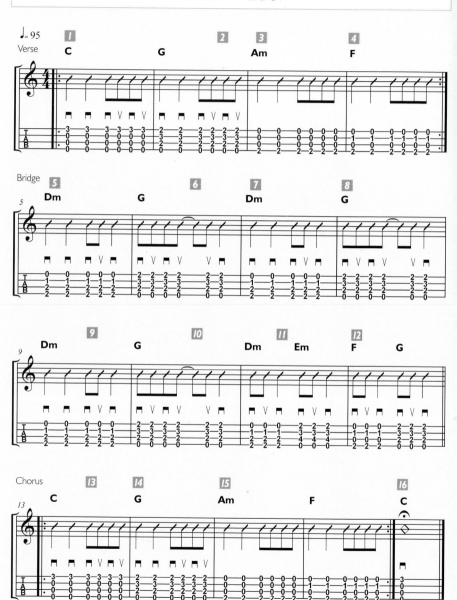

Remember that your strums should not be too wide, since this is likely to lead to an erratic rhythm. This shot illustrates the pick at the end of the first downstrum, finishing just past the soundhole.

When playing upstrums, keep your pick at right angles to the strings, as shown here. The more you move your pick around, the less control you will have over it.

Fret the Am chord with your second finger, making sure that it remains at 90 degrees to the fretboard to avoid damping the third string.

Don't take your second finger off the string; simply add your first finger to the first fret of the second string to form the F chord shape.

Don't forget that for every quarter note downstrum, you will be playing a silent upstrum. Here, the pick returns to position just after playing the first D minor chord.

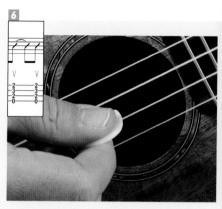

On the third beat you will need to play a silent downstrum to play the tied chord that should be allowed to keep ringing. Raise your pick just off the strings, as demonstrated here.

The D minor chord requires the use of three fretting fingers. Notice how the second finger is squeezed in tightly on top of the third to allow both fingers to get as close to the frets as possible.

Changing from Dm to G is quite tricky because none of the fingers remain on the same strings. Make sure you place each finger tightly behind the frets when fretting the G chord, as shown.

Make sure that your upstrums finish the same distance from the strings as they start. Here, the pick is at the end of the upstrum on beat three, finishing just past the soundhole.

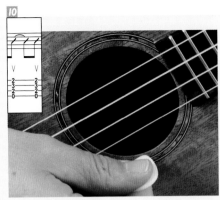

After playing the silent downstrum on beat three, the G chord is sounded with an upstrum, as shown here. Notice how the upstrum starts in exactly the same spot as it would following a regular downstrum.

The chords change pretty quickly in this section, so don't move your fingers too late. Here, the fingers are in position ready to play the Em on beat three, while the picking hand would be playing its upstrum.

When you move quickly back to the F chord from Em, make sure your fingers don't stray too far from the frets. They should be positioned snugly behind them, as shown.

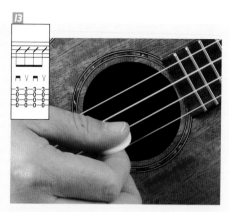

It's very easy to allow your pick to start leaning into the strum when playing consecutive downstrums and upstrums. Always keep your pick at right angles to the strings, as illustrated.

Keep checking that your strumming arm is even and consistent, traveling an equal distance past the strings (just past the soundhole) on both upstrums and downstrums.

Remember to check that your second finger is not touching the third string when fretting the Am chord. As always, keeping the finger at 90 degrees will help to avoid this.

Keep your third finger pressed down hard on the fretboard to allow the final C chord to ring for as long as possible. Releasing the pressure too soon will create unwanted fret buzz.

A promotional shot from Elvis' 1961 film *Blue Hawaii*, proving that only The King could get away with wearing this outfit and still manage to look cool.

Syncopated Strumming

Now you're comfortable with the concept of basic strumming, it's time to learn how to make those rhythm patterns even cooler.

Syncopated rhythms were introduced back in Lesson Six when you learned how to play a silent downstrum. This technique is also featured in the full tune you've been learning in the previous lesson. But playing the occasional silent downstrum is not all there is to playing syncopated strumming patterns. To make our rhythm work even more interesting, offbeats can be accented and highlighted by using percussive string "slaps," rests, and adding sixteenth notes on the offbeats to incorporate reggae flavors. All of these exciting techniques will be broken

down and explained in the exercises that follow. This lesson is all about developing your comping (short for accompaniment) skills and taking your playing into the pro zone. Because the uke is primarily an accompanying tool, the rhythm is just as important (and possibly more so) than the chords being played. In fact, a very simple chord sequence can be mesmerizing in the hands of a skilled musician. So let's get stuck in so you can really get your mates' jaws hitting that floor!

Sixteenth Note Rhythms

It's a good idea to learn how to count sixteenth rhythms correctly before you try playing them. Remember that clapping through the rhythms that you're going to play is an important part of the internalization process. One thing's for sure, "if you can't clap it, you can't play it!"

The old-school name for a sixteenth note is a semiquaver. However most "musos" use the American term because it describes exactly how

long the note is: there are sixteen of them in a bar of regular 4/4 time. So just as we added an "+" to enable us to count eighth notes correctly, so we can add an "e" and "er" to help us to count sixteenth notes, as illustrated below.

EXERCISE I

🎧 Listen to Track 7

This first example introduces the technique of percussive comping where the strings are "slapped" as well as being strummed. This is a very effective comping skill because it can be used, as in this example, to add a backbeat to the groove. The backbeat in all contemporary styles falls on beats two and four; it's where the drummer hits his snare. Keep counting the beat as you play to make sure you're hitting those strings on the right beats!

Bring the side of your hand down onto the strings on the second beat (where you would normally play a downstrum). Allowing the fingers to make contact with the uke's body will add weight to the "slap."

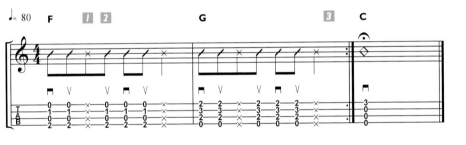

After playing the "slap," your next strum will be played with an up-pick. Here you can see the pick starting the upstrum on the second half of beat two.

To keep the groove going and add momentum, it's a good idea to play a silent upstrum on the fourth beat of both bars.

EXERCISE 2

Listen to Track 8

In this example, you'll learn how adding sixteenth notes can create exciting strumming patterns. Although the picking symbols indicate a down/down/up pattern, you'll actually be playing down/up/down/up on every beat with the first "up" in the sequence played silently (i.e. by lifting the pick off the strings). You'll find it's difficult to change chords quickly enough at the end of each bar; in this situation it's common practice to just strum the open strings while changing shapes. This would not normally be written into the part; it has been added here to indicate exactly where the open strings are played.

As soon as you've played the first F chord with a downstrum, your pick travels back across the strings via a silent upstrum, as illustrated. See how the pick does not make contact with the strings.

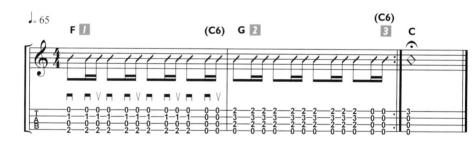

Alternate strumming based on sixteenth notes involves playing a down/up/down/up pattern on every beat. Here, the pick is about to strike the strings with a downstrum on the "+" of the second beat.

The last two strums of each bar play open strings to facilitate a smooth chord change. Here, you can see the fingers have been lifted off the fretboard to allow the open strings to be sounded.

EXERCISE 3

🎧 Listen to Track 9

By removing the first downstrum of the previous strumming pattern, we're left with a cool and funky reggae rhythm. This distinctive rhythm is achieved by playing two sixteenth notes on every offbeat. However, the rests shown between each pair of strums also need to be played. This is achieved by releasing the pressure of your fretting hand, which effectively mutes the chords. Reggae rhythms only work well when you can mute the chord with your fretting hand—that's why the fourth string has not been included in the TAB. Make sure you keep your foot tapping throughout—this will help you to avoid losing the beat.

Although the first chord is sounded on an offbeat, it still needs to be played with a downstrum.

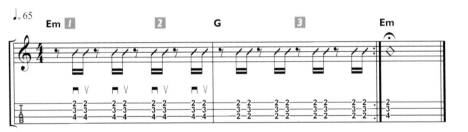

To avoid sounding the fourth string, aim your pick onto the higher strings. Here, you can see the pick making contact with the third string as it plays the last downstrum of the first bar.

To mute the chord on the beat (indicated by the eighth note rests), simply release the pressure of your fretting fingers without taking them off the strings.

lesson 10 Three More Chords

It's very important to keep expanding your chord vocabulary; the more chords you know, the better player you'll be.

In this lesson, we'll be learning three new chord shapes: A major, D major, and G minor. This will bring your chord count up to a total of nine shapes, pretty impressive huh? So give yourself a pat on the back, you're now well on the way to becoming a fully fledged uke player. If you found the previous chords presented no real issues that a little practice wouldn't solve, then you should have no problem with these next shapes. Even if you don't feel completely confident with the chords you've already learned, it's still a good idea to press on and learn new ones.

Sometimes it helps to move on and start the next lesson if you're feeling frustrated; it certainly can't do any harm and it will stop you from getting bored and losing interest. You'll find that as your chord knowledge continues to expand, it will become easier and easier to learn new shapes. And don't worry, there isn't an infinite amount of chords to learn; pretty soon we'll be looking at movable chords and unlocking the secret to playing in any key with just a few basic shapes.

Sorting Chords into Families

As we progress through the book and your chord vocabulary continues to expand, you'll find that it can be quite challenging recalling chords without mixing them up. Obviously you don't want this to happen mid song! Eventually, with time and playing experience, you will know your chord shapes instinctively; you'll be able to recall them without thinking. To speed up this process, start grouping your chords into "families." This not only makes them easier to recall, it makes it easy to identify similarities between them. Let's start with the A major chord in this lesson. If we pair it with the A minor chord from Lesson Seven, you can see that the shapes are very similar; just adding the first finger to the Am transforms it to the A.

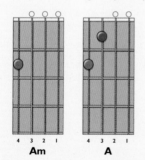

Here's how your chord family list should look so far. Why not keep your own list in a notebook so you can add to it as you progress through the book?

Major Chords:	A	C	D	-	F	G
Major 6 Chords:	-	C6	-	-	-	-
Minor Chords:	Am	-	Dm	Em	-	Gm

EXERCISE 1

A Major

This chord should present no problems at all because it simply adds an extra finger to the A minor shape you already know. It's also a very similar shape to the F major chord, so take care when positioning that first finger. To help you to learn the "sound" of the chord as well as its shape, try alternating between A major and A minor. Simply lift your first finger on and off the strings while keeping your second finger in position on the fourth string. Notice how the major shape has a bright "happy" sound in contrast to the "sad"-sounding minor.

PLAYING A

Keep your first and second fingers at right angles to the fretboard to ensure that they are not damping adjacent strings. Strum the chord slowly just to double check.

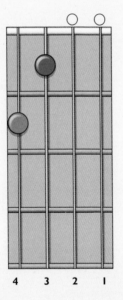

4   3   2   1

D Major

Another easy one for the guitar players out there, this D major shape is the same as an A chord shape on the guitar. Because the fretboard is a lot smaller on a uke, you will need to use the suggested fingering; it's easier to fret this shape using your second, third, and fourth fingers. Just as you did with the previous chord of A major, you should practice alternating between D major and D minor once you've got the shape down. Lift off your fourth finger while you simultaneously place your first finger on the first fret (keeping your remaining fingers in position).

PLAYING D

You'll need to bunch your fingers together quite tightly in order to play three strings on the same fret. Make sure your fourth finger remains behind the second fret and doesn't creep on top of it.

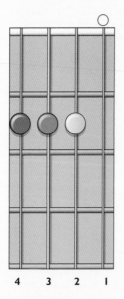

4   3   2   I

G Minor

The final chord for this lesson is G minor. This chord also involves fretting three strings simultaneously but, because each finger is on a different fret, it's a much less compact form. Guitarists will again recognize this distinctive finger pattern as the Dm shape. As with both the previous chords in this lesson, practice alternating between G minor and G major. Changing between the two shapes is a little more involved this time because you'll need to swap the first and second fingers around while keeping your third finger in position.

PLAYING Gm

It's important to make sure that your third finger is not touching the first string when you're forming this shape. Keep your thumb in position, supporting the fingers behind the neck, and keep your fingers as close to 90 degrees as you can.

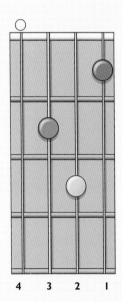

4   3   2   I

PLAY BETTER

To make them easier to remember, all of the chords in this lesson can be paired with the shapes you've previously learned, for instance: A major + A minor (Lesson Seven), D major + D minor (Lesson Seven), and G minor + G major (Lesson Five). Check out the panel called "Sorting Chords into Families" on page 50 for a more detailed explanation.

11 Three Easy Riffs

Who said the uke was only good for strumming? In this lesson, we'll be looking at three riffs that are easy to learn and great fun to play.

In this lesson, you'll learn three distinctly different types of riff: 1) chord based; 2) single note based; and 3) double stop based. These different riff approaches all have one thing in common: rhythm. A riff needs to be based around a short, usually syncopated, rhythmic phrase to make it sound interesting. Chicago blues guitarists like Muddy Waters could turn one chord into a riff just by playing it with a cool rhythm. Because the rhythm of a riff is so important, you should clap through all of these examples before you play them.

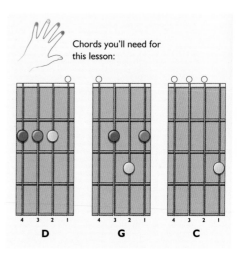

Chords you'll need for this lesson:

D   G   C

Playing Double Stops

What is a double stop? Traditionally used by all stringed instrument players, especially violin and guitar, it's also used to describe this technique on the uke. Double stops can be played on any pair of strings, adjacent or nonadjacent, as the notation below illustrates. They are extremely useful for playing riffs, especially on the guitar. In Exercise Two of this lesson we'll be stealing some of the guitar world's thunder and using double stops to create a cool, rockin' uke riff!

EXERCISE I

◔ Listen to Track 10

The first riff in this lesson is chord based and uses a repeated one-bar rhythm to grab the listeners' attention. Although this riff is in the key of D major, the use of the nondiatonic (i.e. not belonging to the key) chord of C major gives it a distinctive blues-rock vibe. The rhythmic phrasing focuses entirely on the backbeat (beats two and four), giving this riff its strong groove, and making it sound cool even without the "rock band" accompaniment you can hear on the CD.

Keep your arm moving in a constant down/upstrum pattern throughout. Here, we capture the upstrum on the offbeat of beat one.

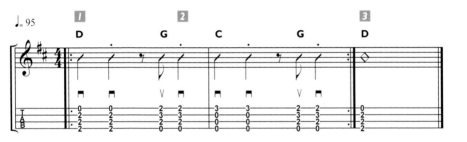

The chords on the second and fourth beat are marked with a staccato dot (see page 59), so you'll need to damp the strings with the side of your picking hand as illustrated to keep them short.

To allow the final chord to ring for its full value, make sure that your fingers fret the notes cleanly (i.e. without touching adjacent strings).

EXERCISE 2

🎧 Listen to Track 11

In complete contrast to the previous riff, this example has a distinctively Celtic vibe, proving just how versatile the uke can be. Although this is a riff comprised of only single notes, the strings should be allowed to ring into each other where possible to achieve a smooth delivery. This piece should be played with constant alternate picking (as indicated above the TAB), so begin your practice well below the tempo indicated (60bpm is a good starting point).

When you're using alternate picking, the arc (or sweep) of your pick should be quite narrow, spanning no more than the strings you're picking. Here, the pick is at the end of the first downstroke, just past the second string.

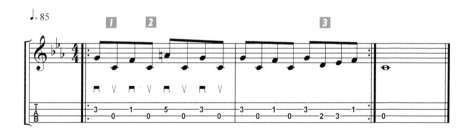

Move your hand up to third position (i.e. with the third finger above the fifth fret) while picking the open C on beat two. You will then be ready to play the A note that immediately follows it.

The low D on beat three of bar two should be fretted with your second finger, leaving your third and first fingers free for the notes that follow. Notice how the third finger is already in position, ready for the next note.

EXERCISE 3

🎧 **Listen to Track 12**

One of the cool features of the uke is that you can play power chords (i.e. the root note plus a fifth, hence the "5" symbol) on the third and fourth strings by simply barring across the frets with one finger. This makes it very easy to play cool sounding riffs like this one. Notice that, although this riff is based entirely on eighth note rhythms, we'll be using downpicks throughout to add more weight and "authority" to the sound. Put simply, this technique will make it "rock"!

To fret the first double stop, lay your first finger flat across the strings, as illustrated. Focus your finger's fretting pressure on the third and fourth strings; this will prevent the first and second strings from sounding.

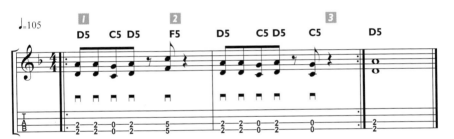

Use your third finger (again, focusing fretting pressure onto the lower strings) to fret the F5 double stop on the third beat. Notice how the hand remains in position to make it easy to return to the second fret in the following bar.

To mute the final C5 double stop in bar two, gently rest your first finger across the second fret as soon as you've picked the strings, as shown.

12 Song 2: The Kingston Shuffle

Test all your new skills with a grooving reggae tune that incorporates syncopated strumming and single note riffs.

There's something about playing reggae rhythms on the uke that just sounds "right." Perhaps it's because Hawaii and Jamaica are both tropical islands. Whatever the reason, it works, so let this tune infuse your playing with some cool tropical island vibes. The parts are based on the way a guitar player would approach a reggae tune. The guitar has two roles to play in a reggae composition: the offbeat "skank," where the chords are played staccato (i.e. short) on the offbeats; and the "link," where the bass players' riff is doubled an octave higher. The comp in the verse section of this tune is based on a reggae skank and so it's ideal for practicing your new

syncopated strumming technique. The chorus section is based on a link line doubling the bass part, and gives you a chance to explore the riffing potential of your instrument. The reggae groove sounds deceptively simple, but because it's completely syncopated, it can be tricky at first. A completely relaxed groove is the secret to making reggae rhythms sound authentic. So why not kick back and imagine yourself relaxing on a tropical beach to get into the vibe.

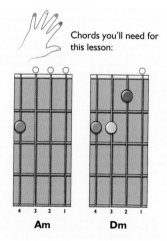

Chords you'll need for this lesson:

Am   Dm

Performance Notes

🎧 **Listen to Track 13, play with Track 14**

There are different opinions as to how reggae should be counted. Some say it should be counted with the skanks on beats two and four. Others consider it to be a slow groove with the skanks on the offbeats and the kick drum on beats two and four. Reggae evolved from Jamaican Rude Boys dancing to ska records at half speed because it was more in keeping with their cool image. For me, that's a good enough reason to count this music the second way—slowly! It's like the famous reply that jazz musician Fats Waller gave when asked exactly what swing was: "Lady, if you gotta ask, you ain't got it!" Don't spend too much time analyzing, try to get inside the music and "feel" it.

Reggae is, like all genres, an acquired taste. It's a rhythmically ambiguous groove that's based entirely on syncopation. If you haven't listened to reggae before, go check some out. If you don't know where to start, listen to anything by Bob Marley, Jimmy Cliff, or Desmond Dekker.

In common with jazz, reggae is frequently played with a swing feel. However, unlike jazz, it's not the eighth notes that are swung but the sixteenth notes. This doesn't change the feel of the skank, but it does affect the phrasing of the link in the chorus. The link is based on sixteenth notes so it must be played with a swing feel. Listen carefully to the bass part when you're playing along with the backing track and try to "lock" with it rhythmically.

Staccato Dot

All of the eighth notes in this piece should be played staccato. This is indicated by the staccato dot above the chords in the verse and below the single notes in the chorus (see over the page). Staccato literally means "detached." In other words staccato chords and notes should be prevented from ringing into each other by muting them to prevent them sounding for their full written value. This creates space in the arrangement; it also makes the skank and link parts sound more rhythmic and percussive.

Staccato chords: **Staccato notes:**

The Kingston Shuffle

♩= 65 swing (sixteenths)

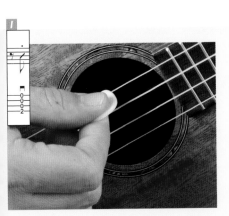

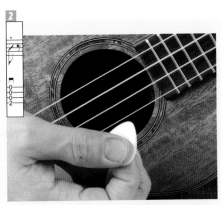

Although offbeat notes are generally played with an upstrum, in reggae they are always played with a downstrum to give them a strong accent. Here you can see the first Am chord is played with a downstrum.

As soon as you've played the first Am chord, bring the edge of your fretting hand palm gently down onto the strings to mute the chord and keep it short.

Fret the Am chord with your second finger, making sure that it remains at 90 degrees to the fretboard to avoid damping the third string.

Don't take your second finger off the string when changing to Dm, simply add your first and second fingers on the second and third strings, as shown.

You'll find it's easier to keep your strumming in time if you add silent downstrums on the start of each beat. Here, the pick is playing a silent downstrum on the first beat.

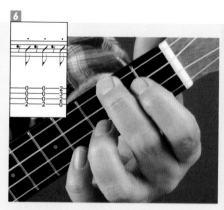

Watch out for that quick G chord that precedes the chorus in bar eight. When you're playing the final Am chord, your first and third fingers should already be in position above the strings, as shown here.

The open third string is played twice on the first beat of the chorus. Make sure you play the second note with an up-pick as indicated in the TAB and illustrated here.

As you position your pick to play the open second string (third note), allow the edge of your thumb to make contact with the lower string to prevent the previous note from ringing on.

Instead of playing the G on the third fret with your third finger, use your first finger as shown. This moves your hand up to third position, keeping your third finger free for the A on beat three.

However, in the second bar the same note should be played with your third finger. That's because the riff descends the second time you play it, so you'll need your first finger to play the F on the first fret.

A dot under a note indicates that it should be played staccato (short). Use the edge of your picking hand thumb to mute open strings; fretted notes are muted by releasing fretting pressure without taking your finger off the string.

The "3" above the notes on beat three indicates a triplet. That's where three eighth notes are played where normally only two would be played. Use downpicks as shown and listen carefully to make sure your rhythm matches the bassline.

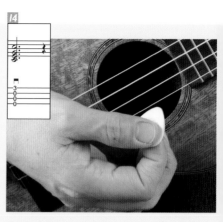

Use your second finger to play the D on the third string, as illustrated here. As soon as you've played the note, release the pressure of your finger to mute the note and keep it short (indicated by the staccato dot under the note).

The final C chord should be muted on the third beat so that it matches the duration of the chord on the backing track. Gently touch the strings with the edge of your picking hand palm, as illustrated.

English indie folk band Noah and the Whale's frontman, Charlie Finn, frequently switches between uke and guitar during the band's live shows.

lesson
13 Barre Chords

Barre chords change everything. Once you've learned a few basic shapes, you'll be able to find any chord you want anywhere on the neck.

Chords you'll need
for this lesson:

D6   **D**

Many people find barre chords a real stumbling block on the guitar; thankfully they're a lot easier to play on the uke. So if the mention of them brings you out in a cold sweat, you've no need to worry, with a little practice you'll soon be playing them with ease. You might wonder what the point of barre chords is when there are so many open chords to choose from. But without barre chords you'd be unable to play in certain keys, and you'd also find it very difficult to play tunes with frequent modulations, such as jazz standards or show tunes. You'd also have limited choices when jamming with other musicians, and you certainly wouldn't be able to accommodate that singer that wants to try the song "just a semitone" higher or lower. So although they are a little more demanding to play than regular open chords at first, once you've got used to the shapes, you'll wonder how you ever managed without them.

PLAY BETTER

Barre chords can be quite tiring to practice for long periods, so don't overdo it. Try mixing them with open chord shapes. Remember that you can also just strum the open strings to play a C6 chord.

D6 Barre Chord

Because the uke is tuned to the chord of C6, when you barre across any fret, you'll be playing a "6" chord. Remember that, unlike the guitar, the root note of a barre shape is not on the lowest string. On the uke, it's the third string that's the key to finding your way when playing barre shapes. So to find out exactly what "6" chord it is you're playing when you barre across the strings, you'll need to identify the note on the third string. Hence our D6 barre chord contains the note D on the third string. If you're unsure of how to find notes on the third string, now is a good time to check back to page 12 for another look at the handy "Instant Note Finder."

PLAYING D6

It's very important to check that all of the notes are ringing clearly in this chord. If they're not, double check your hand position and make sure it looks like this.

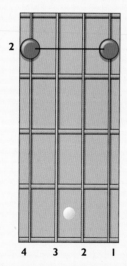

PLAY BETTER

The secret of playing barre chords successfully is entirely dependent on a good fretting hand position. It's all about keeping your thumb behind the neck to support your barring finger. Think of the thumb and first finger as a clamp squeezing together in a pinching action. It's the power of both fingers that's needed to execute sweet sounding barre chords.

EXERCISE 2

D Major Barre Chord

Remember when you learned how to play a simple C major chord back in Lesson Five? All you did was put your third finger on the third fret of the first string and voilà; you were playing C major. It's exactly the same principle here. Add a finger on the first string, three frets higher than the barre, and you'll be playing a straight major chord: in this case D major. However, because we're already using the first finger to barre across the second fret, you'll need to use your fourth finger to fret the higher note. Once you're comfortable with the shape, try moving it around the neck.

PLAYING D

Be careful not to let your first finger angle away from the second fret when you add your fourth finger for this chord. It should remain completely parallel to the fret, as shown.

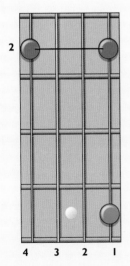

14 The CAGED System

No we're not talking a detention scheme for lack of uke practice; this is a cool approach to chord shapes that could revolutionize your playing.

On the guitar, the "CAGED" system has been helping guitar players to rationalize the guitar neck for many decades. It's so-called because each letter represents the five open "parent" chord shapes. When these chords are converted to movable shapes and then placed in the same key, the shapes lock into each other just like jigsaw pieces, forming one huge chord that spans the whole neck. We can apply this same liberating system to the uke, but only after making one change. Unfortunately, it means that snappy, memorable acronym is transformed into "CAGFD". This is because the E chord shape on the uke is simply a D chord played two frets higher, so it doesn't qualify as a parent shape. The five parent open shapes on the uke are:

C, A, G, F, and D. We've already covered these chords in Lessons Five (page 26) and Ten (page 50), but as a reminder, here are the shapes again for reference.

The next step is to convert these shapes into movable chords that can be played anywhere on the neck. Once this has been done they can be placed in the same key to form one giant C chord that spans the uke neck.

Finally, the diagram opposite illustrates how the fingerboard can be converted to a giant C chord using the CAGFD system. This is not only incredibly useful for finding alternative chord voicings, it can also be applied to arpeggio and scale patterns too.

Chords you'll need for this lesson:

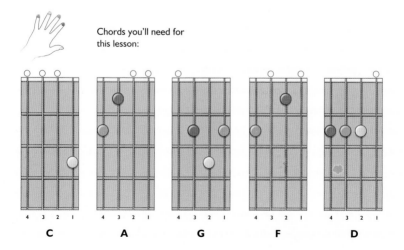

4 3 2 1	4 3 2 1	4 3 2 1	4 3 2 1	4 3 2 1
C	**A**	**G**	**F**	**D**

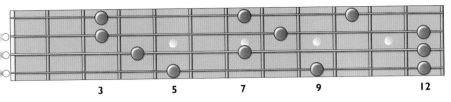

3   5   7   9   12

Giant C Chord

This diagram illustrates the giant C chord shape, created using the five CAGFD forms. The A, G, F, and D chords are converted to C by changing their position on the neck. They can then be placed end to end, interlocking like jigsaw pieces. This system is also useful for learning arpeggio and scale patterns.

Tiny Tim was an eccentric, ukulele-playing singer who had a cult following in the 1960s and 1970s.

Converting to New Keys

It can get mighty confusing when referring to the CAGFD parent chords by their letter names. To alleviate this problem, convert the shapes to numbers, so a "C shape" is shape one, an "A shape" is shape two and so on. Using this system, Exercise One (over the page) would no longer be the confusingly titled C major "A shape," but become C major shape two.

This system makes applying the CAGFD system to other keys a breeze, as long as you always remember to observe the CAGFD sequence. This is obviously easier to apply when dealing with numbers. As an example, when applied to the key of G, the lowest parent shape is an open (shape three) G chord. To maintain the CAGFD sequence, the remaining four shapes would be shape four ("F shape"), shape five ("D shape"), shape one ("C shape"), and finally, shape two ("A shape"). Try applying CAGFD to different keys and you'll soon appreciate how wonderfully logical the system is.

EXERCISE I

C Major as an "A Shape" Chord

To convert any chord to a movable shape, first you'll need to change the fingering to allow the first finger to fret the notes that are currently open strings. The open A chord contains two open notes on the first and second strings. In the chord box, you'll see that the second and third fingers now fret the lower notes that were originally played by the first and second fingers. You'll find it easier to change the fingering of the fretted notes before you convert it to a movable shape and slide it up to the third fret.

PLAYING C MAJOR AS AN "A SHAPE"
Bend the first joint of your first finger slightly to ensure that the tip of the finger is nice and flat across the strings. This will ensure that both notes ring clearly.

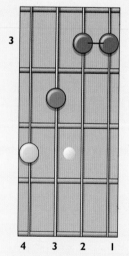

3

4   3   2   1

EXERCISE 2

C Major as a "G Shape" Chord

Because the parent G chord contains only one open string, changing it to a movable shape doesn't involve any barring. However, you will need to do quite a bit of finger swapping in order to free up your first finger. To make this process easier and less confusing, do this with the regular open G shape first. Once you're happy with the shape, you can then slide it up to the seventh fret. Finally, add your first finger on the fifth fret, as shown in the chord box.

PLAYING C MAJOR AS A "G SHAPE"

Because the fourth finger is the weakest finger, you'll need to take extra care when fretting the second string. Keep it as upright as possible to avoid accidentally muting the first string.

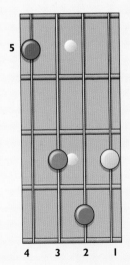

EXERCISE 3

C Major as an "F Shape" Chord

The open F shape is different to all the other parent chord shapes because the fretted notes are separated by open strings. This means that, although there are only two open strings in the chord, converting it to a movable shape involves barring across all four strings. Once again, to free up that first finger you'll need to switch your fingers and use your second and third fingers to play the two fretted notes. Then slide the shape all the way up the neck until your second finger is on the eighth fret. Finally, add the barre across the seventh fret to complete the chord.

PLAYING C MAJOR AS AN "F SHAPE"
Although only the first and third strings are barred, you'll find it's easier to achieve a comfortable hand position when fretting across all four strings, as shown here.

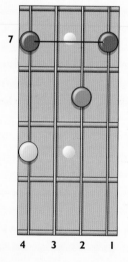

C Major as a "D Shape" Chord

This is the trickiest shape of the four movable parent chords, but only because it needs to be played so high up the neck to play a C chord. As before, always start by converting the original open chord first to make switching fingers less confusing. The D chord has its open note on the first string, so care must be taken to avoid muting this note when you're swapping your fingers around. Once you're happy with the shape, slide it all the way up to the twelfth fret and add your first finger on the tenth fret to form the barre.

PLAYING C MAJOR AS A "D SHAPE"

It's pretty tricky playing this shape high up the fretboard, so make sure you're second, third, and fourth fingers are packed in nice and tight behind the twelfth fret, as illustrated.

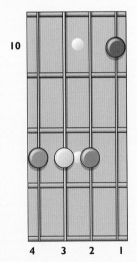

15 Seventh Chords

Seventh chords will add excitement to your music. In this lesson, you'll learn three different shapes for this important chord type.

The dominant seventh chord (to give it it's full "wordy" title) is an extremely useful shape. That's because it's essentially a dissonant chord. Dissonance is what makes music exciting; it creates movement by introducing tension, which is released when a dissonant chord is followed by a nondissonant chord. Traditionally, the dominant seventh chord is resolved to a major or minor chord as a perfect fourth (i.e. four notes) higher. This is what is known as a perfect cadence. You'll instantly recognize this progression when you hear it; it's found in every style of music from Bach to Britney! But seventh chords don't always resolve. Blues musicians frequently leave seventh chords unresolved, and even use them to replace tonic major

and minor chords. Because the blues has had a huge influence on popular music, our ears now accept this sound, so it's difficult for us to appreciate just how discordant early blues tunes must have sounded. No wonder it was referred to as "the Devil's music!" So whatever context it's used in, the dominant seventh is a powerful chord that can't be ignored. In this chapter, you'll not only learn three open chords, but also how to convert them into three movable shapes.

The Ukulele Orchestra of Great Britain dress in the formal attire of a proper orchestra but play ukuleles, and play them superbly well.

Keeping Your Chord Library Organized

Your chord vocabulary will be quite extensive by the time you've completed this lesson. Keeping track of all of these chord types can be difficult, so lets recall how we sorted chords into families back in Lesson Ten. In addition to sorting chords into families, we now need to distinguish between open and movable shapes. To keep things simple, we'll use the numbered shape system explained in the previous lesson. This is where a "C shape" is shape one, an "A shape" is shape two, and so on. You can see that next to the C major chord, the brackets indicate that you now know all five shapes for this chord. In time, you'll be able to fill in the gaps, eventually learning five shapes for every chord.

Chord Tally

Major Chords:	A (o)	-	C (o,2,3,4,5)	D (o,1)	-	F (o)	G (o)
Major 6 Chords:	-	-	C6 (o)	D6 (1)	-	-	-
Minor Chords:	Am (o)	-	-	Dm (o)	Em (o)	-	Gm (o)
Dominant Chords:	A7 (o,3)	B7 (2)	C7 (o)	D7 (2)	-	-	G7 (o)

KEY
open chord type indicated by "o"
movable chord type indicated by CAGFD shape numbers 1–5

C7

This is not only the easiest shape, it is also the most "stable" sounding voicing of the three dominant seventh chords. That is because the root note, C, is the lowest note of the chord (i.e. the open third string). When the root note is the lowest note, it gives the chord more stability so the chord is referred to as being in "root position." This is a very easy shape to convert to a movable barre form, as you can see from the second chord box. Playing this on the second fret produces a shape one D7 chord.

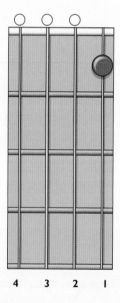

4   3   2   I

PLAYING C7

Use your first finger to fret the note on the first string, ensuring that your finger is placed close to the fret, as shown here.

D7

It's worth converting each new open shape you learn to a movable one straightaway. This is the movable version of a C7 shape. If you look at the relationship between the barre on the D7 chord below and the open strings in the C7 chord on the opposite page, you'll see that the shape is exactly the same. It's important to know where the root note is; in this case it's on the third string. What chord would be created if you moved this shape to the fourth fret?

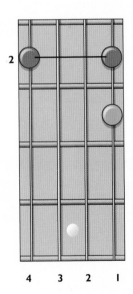

4   3   2   I

PLAYING SHAPE ONE D7

Remember that the key to playing successful barre chords is to support the first finger with your thumb, correctly positioned on the back of the neck.

A7

This chord is another easy one finger shape. However, this chord does not have the root (A) as its lowest note but C♯, which is the major third of the chord. When a chord no longer has its root as the lowest note, it's called an inversion. The mathematics of chord construction are not important here, what is important is that you hear how this chord has a slightly less stable sound when compared to the previous chord. As you can see in the second chord box, the barred version is also an easy shape to play. Playing this on the second fret produces a shape two B7 chord.

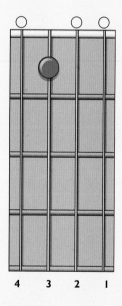

PLAYING A7

Make sure that your first finger is placed cleanly on the fretboard, avoiding contact with the second string by keeping it at a 90 degree angle.

B7

Below you can see the movable version of your new A7 chord shape. By comparing the barre in the B7 chord below with the row of notes formed by the open strings in the A7 chord opposite, you'll see that the shape is exactly the same. The "A shape" seventh chord has its root note on the first (top) string. Try moving the shape around the neck and working out the name of the seventh chord you're playing.

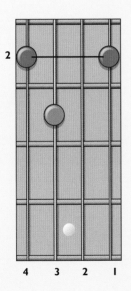

4   3   2   1

PLAYING SHAPE TWO B7
Use your first finger to barre across all four strings, keeping it completely flat, as illustrated. This will ensure that each string rings clearly.

G7

Guitar players will instantly recognize this shape as a D7 chord on the guitar. The characteristic triangular pattern makes it an easy shape to memorize, even if you've never played it before. This chord is also an inversion because its lowest note is the fifth of the chord, D. Once again, don't worry about the maths involved; just play each chord and see if you can hear the subtle differences. Converting this chord to a movable shape involves swapping all your fingers around to free up your first finger; then move the shape two frets higher. You can then add your first finger on the fourth string as shown in the second chord box. Playing the movable shape on the second fret produces a shape three A7 chord.

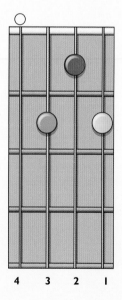

4   3   2   I

PLAYING G7

Keep your second finger as upright as possible when fretting the third string. This will help you to avoid inadvertently muting the second string.

A7

This shape requires no barre when converting it to a movable form. That's because the open G7 shape (see opposite) is formed with three fretted notes, so there's only one open string to be taken care of. Because you'll need to free up your first finger to do this, you'll have to swap your fingers around, as illustrated below. The "G shape" seventh chord has its root note on the fourth (bottom) string. As before, try moving the shape around the neck and working out the name of the chords you play.

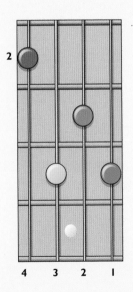

PLAYING SHAPE THREE A7

Ensure that all of your fingers are positioned snugly behind their respective frets, as shown. This will enable you to produce a clear, authoritative sound.

lesson

16 Song 3: Access All Areas

This exciting original arrangement demonstrates how you can start exploring those higher frets using just one movable shape.

The last three lessons have focused entirely on chords. That's because without a good chord vocabulary and an understanding of movable shapes, you will not be able to capitalize on one of the uke's greatest strengths: accompaniment. So in this lesson they'll be no new chords; instead you'll get the chance to apply your new skills and start using some of the shapes you've learned in the previous lessons. There are only two types of barre chord used in this song, shape one (used throughout the verse) and shape two (used for B♭7 and A♭7 in the chorus). These have been mixed with more familiar

open shapes so you don't have to worry about wrestling with two many new chords. The song is written in the key of D♭, a key that would be impossible using open chord shapes alone. You can of course use a capo to play in awkward keys, but this creates its own problems if the song modulates (i.e. changes key) as this one does. But most importantly this tune gets you playing barre chords. It's important to start using new skills as soon as possible; if you don't apply new techniques to real playing situations, they will be quickly forgotten.

Chords you'll need for this lesson:

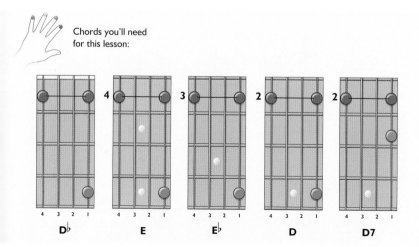

Performance Notes

🎧 **Listen to Track 15, play with Track 16**

Don't be put off by all those unfamiliar chord symbols in the first couple of bars—they'll all be played with just one shape! That's the beauty of movable chord shapes; they make seemingly tricky chord sequences a breeze. Another strength of movable shapes is that they make it easy to "play" rests. There's no tricky damping of open strings to worry about: you simply release the pressure of your fretting hand and all the strings are instantly silenced. This makes playing rhythmic accompaniments, like the tune over the page, very easy.

The key to successful string damping is keeping your fingers in contact with the strings at all times. This not only ensures that the strings remain silent, it also keeps the chord shape intact so you don't have to reposition your fingers.

You'll notice in the verse section that each chord is played on a different fret. Because you've so far only played open shapes, you might think that this would take a lot of practice. But because you'll use just one shape to play all of the chords, it's actually incredibly easy. Starting with the sequence in the first two bars, form the shape one D♭ chord on the first fret. To change to the E chord, simply release the pressure of your fingers (but keep the shape intact) and slide it up to the fourth fret. Once it's in position above the frets, reapply fretting pressure and you've made the change. The shape is then moved down to the third fret and finally the second fret to form the E♭ and D chords respectively. When changing, make sure that your fourth finger remains in position; there should always be two clear frets between the barre (first finger) and the fourth finger.

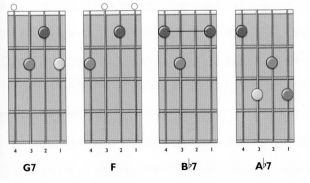

G7   F   B♭7   A♭7

Access All Areas

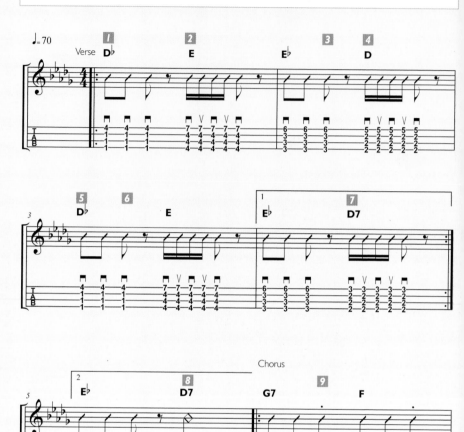

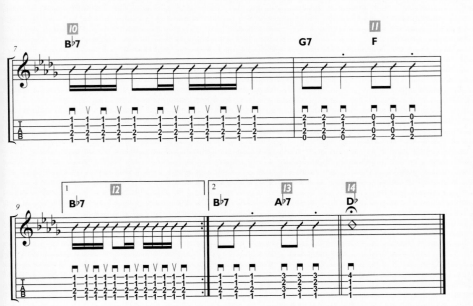

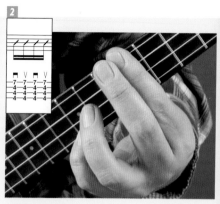

It's important to make sure that your first finger is just behind the first fret and not on top of it when forming the D♭ chord. You can also add your second finger for extra support, as shown.

To change to the E chord, release the pressure of your fretting hand and slide the chord shape up to the fourth fret, making sure that the two-fret-gap between the first and fourth fingers is retained.

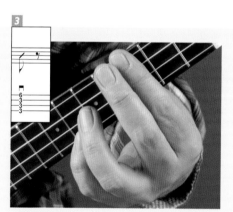

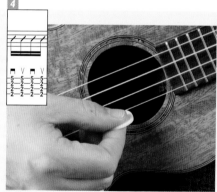

To make sure you play the rest on the "+" of beat two, release the pressure of your fretting hand as soon as you've strummed the third E♭ chord.

You'll be using sixteenth note strumming throughout this piece, so you only use upstrums when playing sixteenth note rhythms. Here the pick is captured playing an upstrum on the second sixteenth (the "e") of beat three.

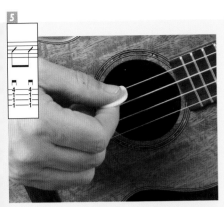

Don't be tempted to use upstrums on offbeats. Stick to the strumming pattern indicated above the TAB. Here, you can see a downstrum is being correctly applied to the D♭ chord on the "+" of beat one.

As soon as you've released the pressure of your fretting hand, slide the chord shape up to the fourth fret. This image captures the movement mid-slide with the shape moving up the strings to its destination fret.

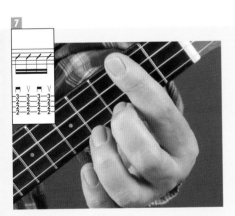

In the fourth bar, the D7 chord replaces the D chord. Keep your first finger snug against the second fret and fret the single note on the third fret with your second finger as shown here.

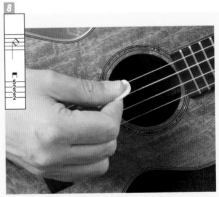

To allow space for the drum fill, a single D7 chord preempts the chorus at the end of the second time bar. Use a downstrum as indicated, making sure that your pick sweeps evenly across all four strings.

To maintain the sixteenth note strumming pattern in the first bar of the chorus, add a silent downstrum on the "+" of beats two and four. Here, the pick plays a silent downstrum, lifted just clear of the strings.

To avoid damping the second string, keep your second finger at 90 degrees to the strings when fretting the B♭ chord, as illustrated here.

To facilitate a smooth chord change, keep your first finger on the second string when changing to the F chord. Here, you can see the second and third fingers have been released but the first finger remains in position.

To play the rhythm for the B♭7 chord correctly, you'll need to play a silent upstrum on the "e" of the second beat, as shown.

The A♭7 chord in the second time bar is a shape three chord. In other words, it's the G7 shape played a fret higher, with the first finger added on the fourth string.

For a quick, smooth change from A♭7 to the final D♭ chord, flatten your first finger across the strings and simultaneously slide your fourth finger one fret higher. Remember, it's always easier to change shapes when you keep your fingers in contact with the strings.

Repeat Bars

First and second time endings are used to notate repeated sections when a different ending is required on the second playing. A bracket is placed over the relevant bar (or bars) to indicate which section is "jumped" on the repeat. So, in the example below, you would play the first two bars as a normal repeat. On the second playing, you would "jump" over the first time bar and proceed straight to the second time bar, i.e. staying on the C chord and omitting the G7. Both the verse and the chorus sections of this tune incorporate first and second time endings.

lesson 17 Pentatonic and Blues Scales

These scales can be used to write melodies and riffs, play solos, or simply to add fills between chords—find out how in this lesson.

As its name suggests, the pentatonic scale consists of five notes. It comes in two basic varieties: major and minor. Adding an extra note to the minor scale creates a third variation, and this six-note scale is called the blues scale because of its popularity with blues guitarists. All three of these scales are extremely useful for creating riffs, melodies, and solos. These scales are widely used in many different styles of music by players of all instruments; they are invaluable to all musicians because they provide a foolproof note pool for improvising.

Each pentatonic scale is essentially a condensed version of the parent major or minor scale, but with the problem notes removed. So the major pentatonic contains no fourth or seventh intervals, while the minor pentatonic contains no second or sixth intervals; it is these intervals that can sound like "bum notes" in the hands of an inexperienced player. The blues scale adds the dark and mysterious ♭5 interval to the minor pentatonic, expanding its creative potential and giving it an instantaneous blues/rock vibe.

Pearl Jam's Eddie Vedder demonstrates how to kill time in the airport departure lounge by getting in a bit of busking before leaving for his hols!

Scale Boxes

Scale boxes, just like chord boxes, are very simple to read; it's just like looking down on the uke neck while you're playing. The color coding for scales is different than previously used in chord boxes. That's because it's important to identify the root note of the scale. Root notes are black, while scale notes are red; fingering is now indicated by the number inside the fret marker dots. Because of the uke's reentrant tuning (i.e. with the lowest string being tuned to a high G), it is common practice to play scales on the top three strings only. Spend some time getting acquainted with these shapes before you move on to the examples.

Scales you'll need for this lesson:

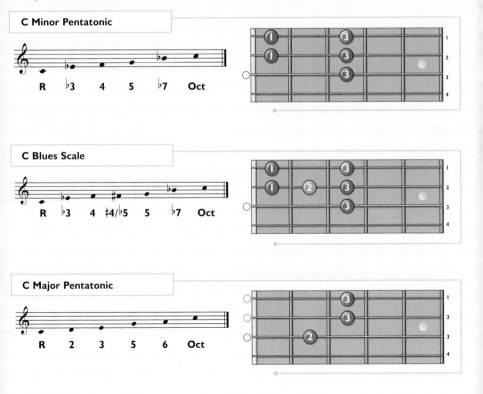

🎧 Listen to Track 17

Although all those sixteenth notes might look
a little scary, this example is actually quite easy
to play once you've got it "under your fingers."
It also demonstrates how you can play a lot
more notes with just one octave of a five-
note scale than you might think. The picking
directions above the TAB indicate that strict
alternate sixteenth note picking should be used
throughout. As always start your practice slowly,
working on each bar separately.

*To quickly fret the B♭ at the start of the second
beat, flatten your first finger across the string as
soon as you've played the F that preceded it. This
should leave the tip of your first finger touching
the second string and keep it muted.*

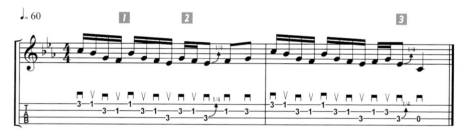

*Exactly the same technique (called finger rolling)
should be used for the G on the start of the third
beat, this time using your third finger, as shown.*

*The penultimate note in the second bar is marked
with an arrow and a "1/4" symbol. This indicates a
quarter tone bend should be played by pushing the
third string toward the second string, as shown.*

EXERCISE 2

🎧 Listen to Track 18

The blues scale is ideal for creating powerful riffs, as this example illustrates. Rock guitarists have been using this scale to create iconic riffs for decades. And although it only contains six notes, the permutations are endless once you add rhythm into the mix. Since the smallest note value here is a sixteenth note, sixteenth note alternate picking should be used throughout, as indicated above the TAB.

Because the first note is marked with a staccato dot, it should be muted to keep it short. This can be achieved by gently touching the string with your second fretting hand finger, as illustrated.

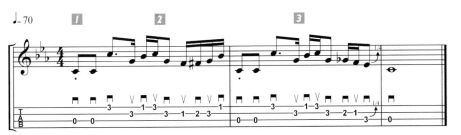

Use your third finger to move quickly from C to G on the third beat by starting with the finger flat across the first string, as shown. When you lift your finger to its normal fretting position, it will "roll" onto the second string while simultaneously muting the first.

In the second bar, make sure you play the first G on the second string with an up-pick, as illustrated.

EXERCISE 3

🎧 Listen to Track 19

Picking out a melody, or adding a fill between strummed major chords, is easy once you've learned the major pentatonic shape. This example shows how a simple melody with a strong Celtic flavor can be tastefully punctuated with C chords by strumming the chord at the start of each bar. This is an extremely effective technique for playing unaccompanied melodies on the uke.

While you're picking the open second string on the last sixteenth note of beat one, move your third finger off the first string and into position above the second string, ready to fret the G that follows.

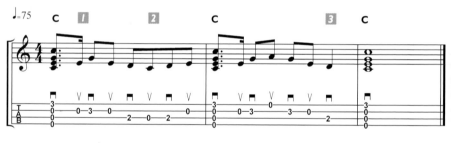

Although sixteenth note picking is used on the first beat, we'll be using alternate eighth note picking for the remainder of the melody notes. Here you can see an up-pick is used to sound the open third string on beat three.

While playing the final D with your second finger, move your third finger in position ready for the final C chord. This will allow you to hold the D for its full value, without compromising the chord change.

Taylor Swift playing her uke with ornate figured top on the opening night of her USA tour in 2011. Note how she's using a strap to keep the uke in place.

18 Introducing Fingerpicking

Use fingerpicking techniques to transform a simple chord sequence into a hypnotic, rhythmic accompaniment.

Using the thumb and fingers to pluck the strings is called fingerpicking; it's an exciting technique that opens up a whole new world of possibilities. But don't panic! We're not talking strict classical fingerstyle as applied to the guitar; instead we'll be focusing on the more relaxed technique that was pioneered by guitar and banjo players in early folk and country music. In this lesson, we'll be applying this easy technique to play arpeggiated chords. An arpeggiated chord occurs when the notes of the chord are sounded individually (ascending or descending) as opposed to being strummed simultaneously with a pick. Although it is also possible to play arpeggiated chords using regular pick technique, it is much easier to do this by using the thumb, first, and second fingers of your picking hand. Because of the reentrant tuning system used on the uke, beautiful harp-like sequences can be easily achieved with just a simple picking pattern. The chords in these examples are all simple open shapes to allow you to concentrate on getting your picking hand together.

Fingerpicking Basics

There are no hard and fast rules regarding this style, but generally you should use your thumb to play the third and fourth strings, your index finger to play the third string, and your middle finger to play the second string. Because the uke only has four strings, you'll find that three fingers are all you need to play cool picking patterns.

Finger Names

Traditional Spanish names are used to name the picking hand fingers—using numbers would create confusion with the fretting hand.

p (*pulgar*) = thumb
i (*indice*) = index
m (*medio*) = middle

Picking hand position

The photo below illustrates an ideal picking hand position. Keep your hand suspended above the strings with the thumb parallel to the third string. Your index and middle fingers should be maintained in a clawlike shape above the second and first strings respectively. This will enable you to pick the strings without moving your fretting hand, and also ensures that each finger remains above its relevant string.

EXERCISE I

🎧 **Listen to track 20**

This first example is based on an easy ascending/descending picking pattern starting with your thumb (*p*) on the third string. One of the great advantages of fingerstyle playing is that you don't always need to fret the full chord. So because no notes are played on the fourth string, the Am can be played using only the top three open strings while the Dm requires only the use of your first and second fretting hand fingers. The *p*, *i*, and *m* finger indications are traditionally placed next to the relevant note in the upper stave, as in all the examples here.

As soon as you've picked the first note with your thumb (p), it should return to its default position above the third string. You'll find this is easiest to achieve when using a circular picking motion.

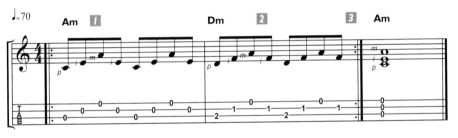

Use just the tip of your finger to pick the strings. Here you can see the middle finger (m) picking the top string with the thumb (p) and index finger (i) nicely in position above their respective strings.

The ending chord is sounded by picking all three strings simultaneously. This shot shows all three fingers (p, i, and m) in position on the strings immediately before playing the final chord.

🎧 Listen to Track 21

Don't be put off by the unusual looking time
signature (12/8) at the start of this piece. This
is a very natural rhythm that you will have heard
many times before. As always, listen to the
CD before you start working on each exercise;
this will help you to fully understand the
rhythmic content. 12/8 time allows the use
of three eighth notes per beat; this results in
a hypnotic rhythmic pattern that's great for
ballads and slower tunes. Most electronic
metronomes can also be set to provide a
"triplet" click that you will find more helpful
than a regular four-beat pulse when practicing.

*Always keep your hand hovering above the strings
with each finger in its default position. Here the
thumb (p) strikes the third string to sound the first
note while the index (i) and middle (m) fingers
remain in their correct position.*

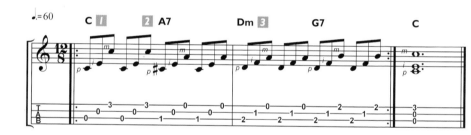

*As you're playing the first C chord, your first
finger should already be in position above the
third string ready to fret the lowest note of the
A7 chord that follows.*

*Don't waste energy fretting notes you won't be
playing. Hence the Dm chord omits the second
finger on the fourth string, since the fourth string is
never played.*

EXERCISE 3

🎧 **Listen to Track 22**

The reentrant tuning of the uke makes it easy to play cool harp-like accompaniments with just a simple repeated picking pattern. To achieve this, the thumb has to alternate between the third and fourth strings, as in this example. Because of this, you'll find this pattern will take a little more time to learn than the previous examples, so it's a good idea to practice it with open strings before you add the Gm and C7 chord shapes. As always, start your practice nice and slowly, working on each bar separately well below the final tempo indication given.

As you're picking the second note, G, with your index (i) finger, move your thumb (p) into position above the fourth string, as illustrated.

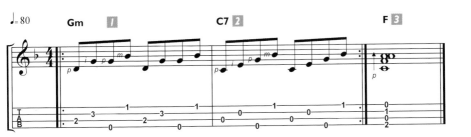

When changing to the C7 chord, keep your first finger firmly in position on the first fret while lifting the second and third fingers off the strings.

To play the final F chord, simply brush your thumb (p) across all four strings. Here, you can see the thumb at the start of its downstrum, just as it makes contact with the fourth string.

19 Picking Patterns

In this lesson, you'll be learning three essential techniques that will enable you to create your own super-slick picking patterns.

In the previous lesson, you discovered that, by using your fingers instead of strumming with a pick, it is possible to pick out chord notes individually to create arpeggiated chord sequences. In this lesson you'll be augmenting these basic skills with three essential techniques that will take your fingerpicking to the next level, making your playing sound slick and professional. The three examples in this lesson will focus

on pinching, the use of hammers and pull-offs, and banjo roll picking. Although none of these techniques are specific to the ukulele, they work exceptionally well and can be used as a basis for accompaniments or solo performances. The uke's reentrant tuning also makes it easy to create complex sounding parts with ease when the high tuned fourth string is included in picking patterns.

Keep Checking that Picking Hand

It's really important to maintain good picking hand technique. So before you play anything, just double check that your picking hand is in the right position. Suspend your hand above the strings with your thumb parallel to the third and

fourth strings and your index and middle fingers forming a clawlike shape above the second and first strings respectively. This will enable you to pick the strings quickly and accurately.

When you're pinching two strings simultaneously as in Exercise One, it's important to make sure that the notes are balanced. To do this you'll need to pick both strings with an equal amount of force. Here, the thumb and index finger are in position, ready to pinch the third and first strings simultaneously. The pinching action should be gentle but firm to avoid producing an unpleasant, overpicked twanging sound.

In order to play banjo rolls effectively (as in Exercise Three), it's very important to keep your hand steady with your thumb (p), index finger (i), and middle finger (m) placed directly above their "home" strings at all times. Here, the thumb is picking the third string while the index and middle fingers are poised and ready above the second and first strings respectively.

EXERCISE I

🎧 Listen to Track 23

This short, classical etude-style example
demonstrates the versatility of pinch picking.
The thumb (p) and index finger (i) pick out the
double stops on the second and fourth strings.
Between each double stop, the thumb also picks
the open third string. It's important to allow
the fretted notes to continuously ring. This is
achieved by maintaining fretting hand pressure
throughout, only releasing the strings when
changing to a new double stop. The *rit* is an
abbreviation of *ritardando* (see page 189) and is
featured in bar three.

*It's important to keep the tips of your fretting fingers
at 90 degrees to the fretboard throughout. This will
keep them clear of the third string to ensure that it
is not damped and rings clearly.*

*When pinching, aim to keep your thumb (p) almost
parallel with the stings and your index (i) finger
curled in a pincer shape.*

*Fret the final double stop at the end of bar three by
barring across the strings with your first finger. Allow
the notes to continue ringing while you add the E on
the third string with your second finger.*

🎧 Listen to Track 24

In complete contrast to the previous example, this simple minor key riff uses hammer-ons and pull-offs to create a hypnotic Celtic-style accompaniment. By adding hammer-ons and pull-offs in this way, sixteenth notes can be added without disrupting the basic picking pattern, which is just a simple alternating p, i, p, m sequence. It's very easy to rush hammer-ons and pull-offs; they need to be played in time to sound effective, so start your practice well below the final tempo indicated and tackle each bar separately, making sure you understand the rhythmic content before you start playing.

Rather than fretting the chord notes separately, you'll find that it's much easier if you hammer-on both the first and second fingers at the start of bar one. This image shows the fingers immediately before being "hammered" into position.

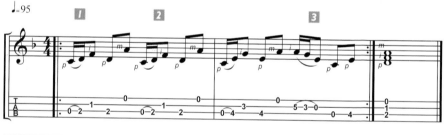

Once the chord shape has been fretted, keep your first finger in position on the second string while you hammer your second finger onto the third string on beat three of the first bar.

To execute pull-offs cleanly and accurately, release your fingers quickly with a sideways flicking motion. This image illustrates the pull-off on beat three (bar two) with the third finger already released and the first finger still on the third fret.

EXERCISE 3

🎧 **Listen to track 25
(60bpm and 80bpm)**

The banjo roll, as its name suggests, is a technique much loved by banjo players. It can be used to create exciting syncopations with just a simple repeated picking pattern, as in this example. To demonstrate the effectiveness of the technique, you'll hear the example at two tempos on the CD, first at 60bpm, then at 80bpm. However, it's important to play this slowly at first to ensure that you're picking evenly and consistently. The accents in the notation illustrate the syncopation created by repeating the three-note pattern.

Fret the first C chord by barring across the first and second strings with your first finger. Make sure that your second finger isn't touching the second string and preventing it from sounding.

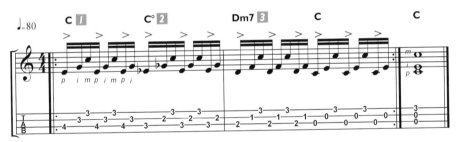

To change to the second chord (C diminished), slide your first and second fingers down the strings one fret and then refret the first string with your third finger...

...you can then slide your first and second fingers down one more fret (keeping the third finger in position) to form the Dm7 chord shape.

lesson

20 Song 4: Bring on Sundown

Astound and amaze your friends with this cool 12-bar blues arrangement designed to showcase your new fingerpicking skills.

The 12-bar blues is the most ubiquitous chord sequence in popular music. So when musicians get together, regardless of what instrument or style of music they play, it is usually the first thing that's suggested for getting the jam session going. Many auditions are also judged on a candidate's ability to play a convincing 12-bar improvisation, whether it's a metal band looking for a guitar hero or a jazz quintet searching

for a virtuoso horn player. Because this is such an important chord sequence, it had to be included in this book, so in this last lesson you'll learn how to strum, create riffs, and play licks in authentic blues style. Although the blues has been popular with guitar players for well over a century, the world has yet to meet its first uke blues "king." So who knows, this could be your first step toward claiming that crown!

Letting the Notes Ring On

To avoid over-complication when writing, sustained notes or passages are indicated by a "let ring" instruction between staves. When you see this instruction, hold the chord notes down (or allow open strings to continue ringing) for the duration indicated (usually by a

dotted bracket). In the example below, the first C major chord would be played as individual notes (i.e. an arpeggio). In the second bar, the notes would be allowed to ring into each other (i.e. an arpeggiated chord).

Arpeggio   Arpeggiated chord

let ring - - - - - - - - - - - - - - - - - -

Strumming the Blues

This arrangement has been specifically designed to showcase your fingerpicking skills. But what if you want to just strum the chords to accompany another instrument or vocalist? That's even easier! Back in Lesson Five you learned your first three chords, C, F, and G. You also learned that these were the chords of I, IV, and V in the key of C major. The blues progression consists of nothing but the chords I, IV, and V, so it's a very easy sequence to transpose to different keys. The only difference is that all of the chords are usually played as dominant seventh chords, not straight majors. The dominant seventh contains the dark and ominous tritone interval (also

referred to as "flat five"). This interval was known as the diabolos in music during the middle ages, probably why the blues was originally referred to as "the devil's music."

It's very easy to improvise over a 12-bar blues progression. You need just one scale: the minor pentatonic. As long as the minor pentatonic starts on the tonic note (i.e. for a blues in C, play C minor pentatonic), then it will fit over all three chords in the sequence. All of the single note riffs and licks in this piece were created using the C minor pentatonic scale. In the library section of this book you'll find a useful resource that lists major and minor pentatonic scales in every key.

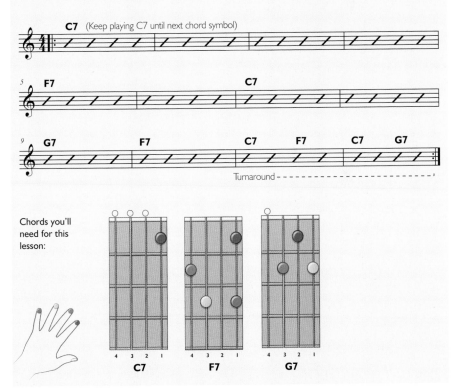

Bring On Sundown

The arrow symbol in the TAB indicates that the first note should be bent slightly sharp (i.e. a quarter tone bend). This is achieved by fretting the note firmly with your first and second fingers and bending the string so that it moves toward the second string.

The single notes on the first and second strings are played with your thumb (p) and index finger (i). This image illustrates the second string being played with the thumb on the second beat. Notice how the index finger is in position above the first string.

The last two notes in bar one are picked with your index finger (i). This shot illustrates the finger returning to repick the string immediately after playing the B♭ on the first fret.

Play the hammer-on on the second string by fretting the F on the first fret with your first finger. Keep the finger in position while you bring the second finger firmly down onto the third fret (without repicking the string).

5

Keep your second finger in position as you move your first finger onto the first string to play the B♭. This will not only produce a more legato delivery, it also avoids having to immediately refret the note when you return to it.

6

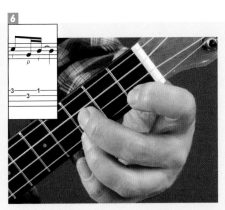

As you fret the high C on the third fret with your third finger, keep your first and second fingers in position for the two notes that quickly follow.

7

The C chord is played by picking the top three strings simultaneously. Use your thumb (p), index finger (i), and middle finger (m), as illustrated.

8

The banjo roll should be played continuously throughout bars five and six. Keep your picking hand steady with the thumb and fingers as close to the strings as possible. Remember that only your fingers should move, not your hand.

At the end of the sixth bar, your thumb (p) moves across to pick the second string. Your index (i) finger should also be in position above the first string, as shown.

Fret the first pair of double stops using your second finger on the third string and your third finger on the first string, as shown...

...this will allow you to keep your second finger on the third string as you slide up to play the second pair of double stops. Use your first finger as shown to fret the first string.

As the double stops climb to the fifth fret, you can revert to the original fingering with your second finger still on the lowest string, as shown here.

Play the double stops by picking the third string with your thumb (p), and the first string with your index finger (i). Note the pincer shape that the fingers form; this is the optimum picking position for playing double stops.

Fret the second pair of double stops in this bar using your second finger on the third string and your first finger on the first string, as shown here.

To play the first four notes of this final minor pentatonic lick, you will need to move up to third position (i.e. with your first finger on the third fret). Play the first note ($E\flat$) with your fourth finger.

On the second beat of bar thirteen you will need to perform a swift position shift back to first position. After playing the preceding note G on the third fret with your first finger, move your hand quickly to allow your third finger to fret the C on the same fret, as shown.

Allow the open third string to continue to ring as you pick the first and second strings with your index finger (i) and middle finger (m). These should also be plucked simultaneously, as shown here.

Pentatonic Scale Library

Notation Guide

Open position (first fret) scale box:

KEY

- O = open string (root note) played
- O = open string (scale note) played
- O = "blue note" occurring as an open string
- ● = root note
- ● = scale note
- ● = "blue note" added to minor pentatonic to create blues scale
- ●–● = barre or semibarre

Scale box starting at the third fret:

Numbers in the fret markers indicate suggested fretting hand fingering

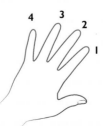

Numbers in the fret markers correspond with the digits of your fretting hand, as depicted.

This resource section will enable you to find any major pentatonic, minor pentatonic, or blues scale, quickly and easily, in any key. Two shapes are given for each scale; the first starting in the lowest available neck position, and the second "bolting on" above, to provide access to notes higher up the fretboard. Notes are color coded (see key opposite) to make it easy to quickly identify those essential root notes. Because of the uke's reentrant tuning, the fourth string has not been included in any of the scale patterns; this would simply duplicate notes found on the higher strings and make the patterns confusing to play. The "blue notes" have also been identified in the blues scale patterns since these are primarily used as a passing note between scale tones. This also makes it easier to see where this "extra" note has been added to the corresponding minor pentatonic scale. You'll find that this section of the book will become a useful resource, invaluable for creating cool licks, solos, riffs, and fills between chords.

PRACTICE TIPS

Learn both shapes in sequence for all keys. Once you've done this try playing "along the strings." This will enable you to move smoothly between the two patterns.

Learn the open strings available in any key. These notes can be included when playing chords to create fills between them.

Learn the corresponding CAGFD chord shape for each scale shape. This is the key to achieving total fretboard fluency.

C Major Pentatonic

Shape One

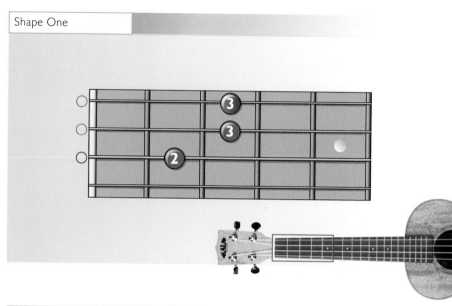

Shape Two

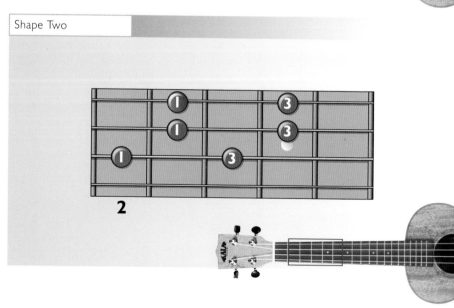

C Minor Pentatonic

Shape One

Shape Two

3

C Blues Scale

Shape One

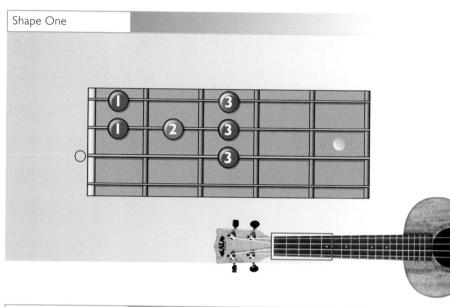

Shape Two

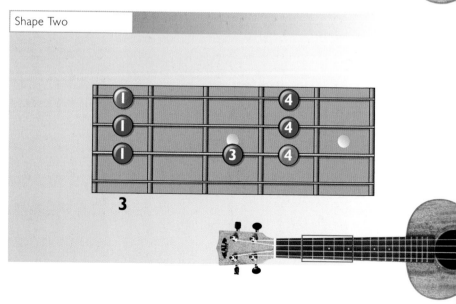

C♯ Major Pentatonic

Shape One

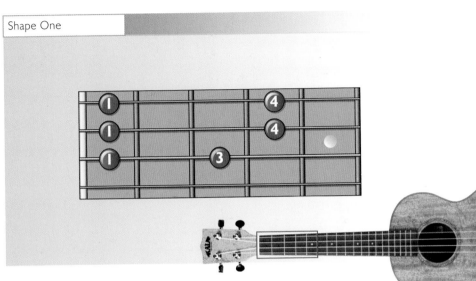

Shape Two

C# Minor Pentatonic

Shape One

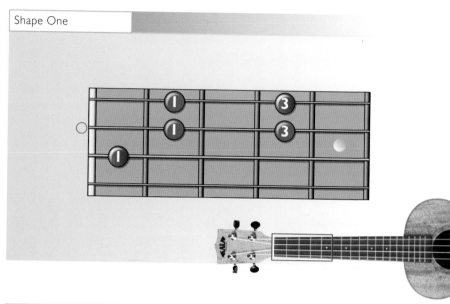

Shape Two

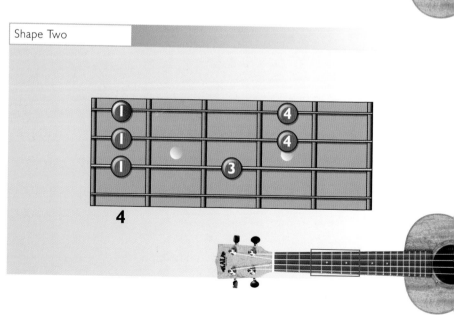

C# Blues Scale

Shape One

Shape Two

4

D Major Pentatonic

Shape One

Shape Two

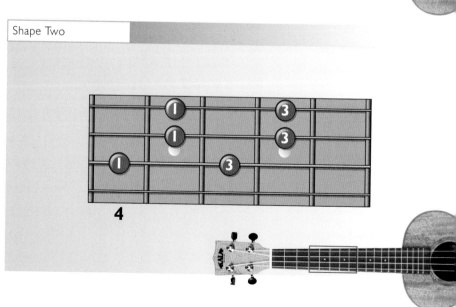

D Minor Pentatonic

Shape One

Shape Two

D Blues Scale

Shape One

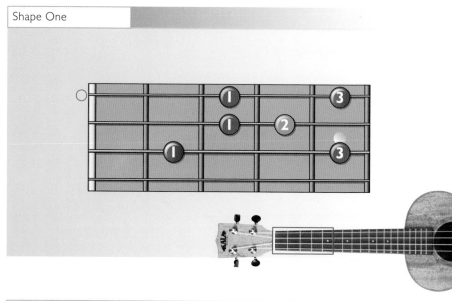

Shape Two

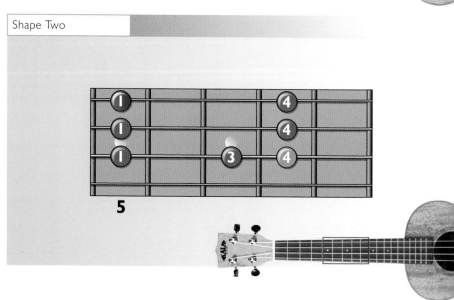

E♭ Major Pentatonic

Shape One

Shape Two

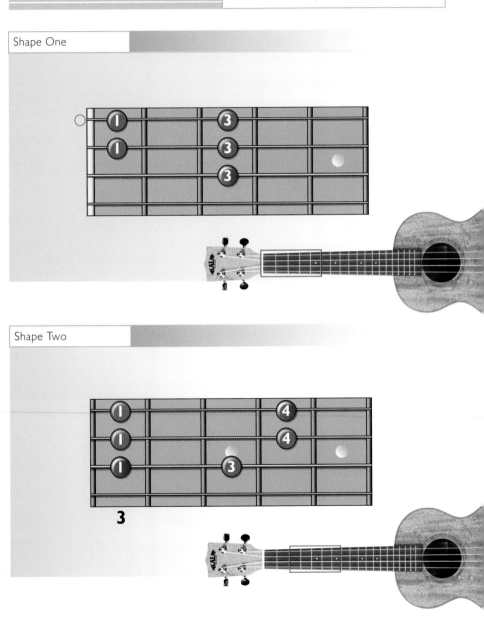

3

E♭ Minor Pentatonic

Shape One

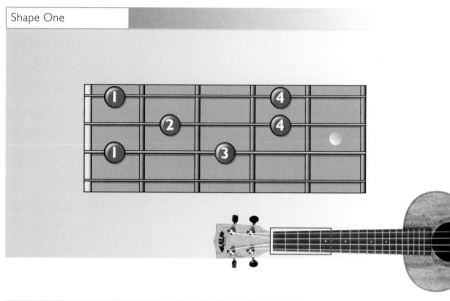

Shape Two

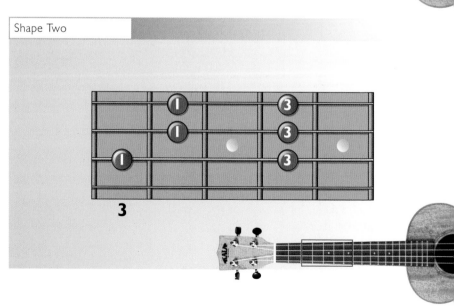

E♭ Blues Scale

Shape One

Shape Two

E Major Pentatonic

Shape One

Shape Two

4

E Minor Pentatonic

Shape One

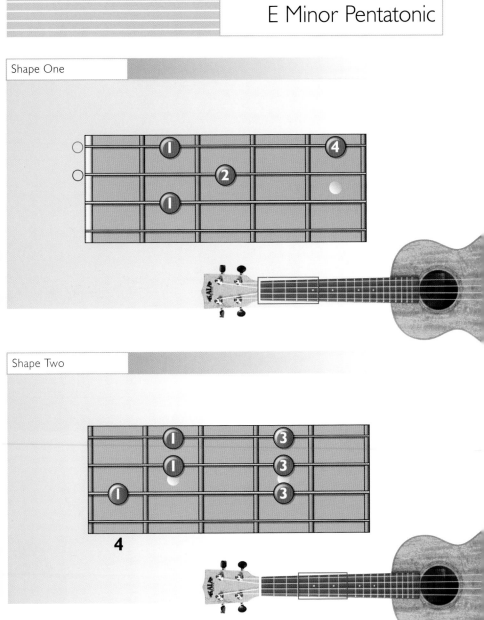

Shape Two

E Blues Scale

Shape One

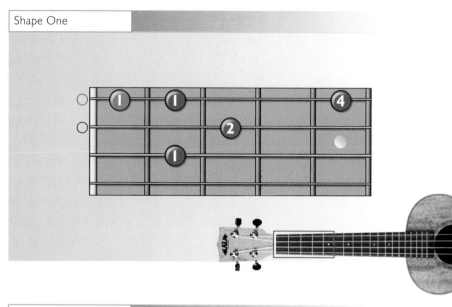

Shape Two

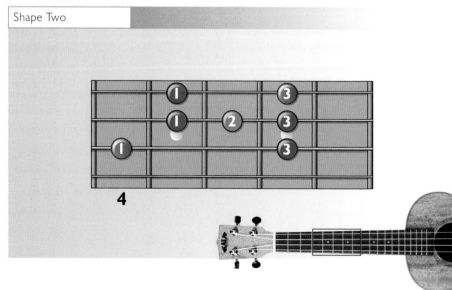

F Major Pentatonic

Shape One

Shape Two

2

F Minor Pentatonic

Shape One

Shape Two

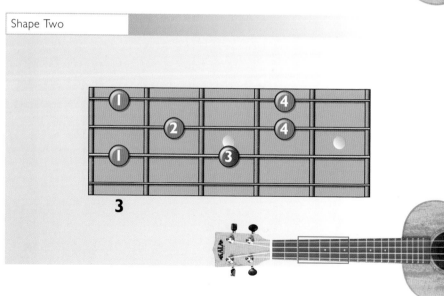

F Blues Scale

Shape One

Shape Two

2

F# Major Pentatonic

Shape One

Shape Two

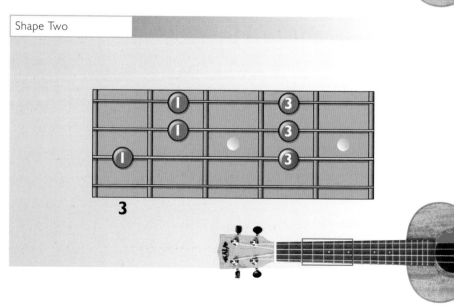

F♯ Minor Pentatonic

Shape One

Shape Two

F♯ Blues Scale

Shape One

Shape Two

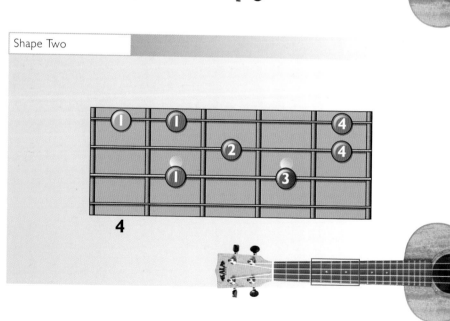

G Major Pentatonic

Shape One

Shape Two

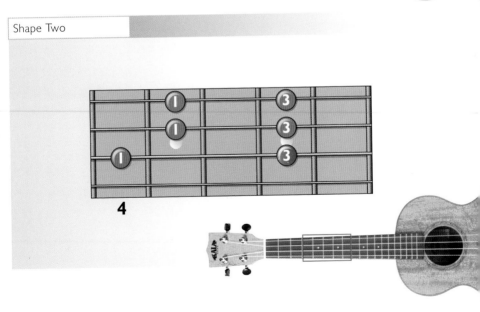

G Minor Pentatonic

Shape One

Shape Two

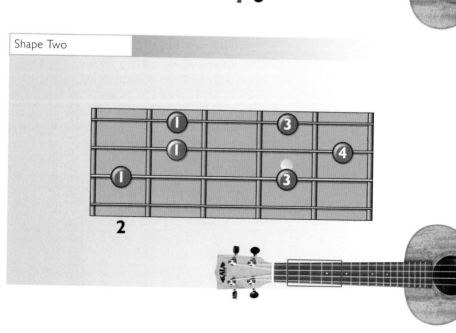

G Blues Scale

Shape One

Shape Two

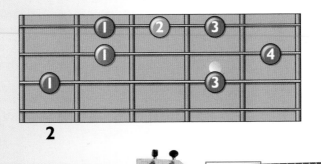

2

A♭ Major Pentatonic

Shape One

Shape Two

A♭ Minor Pentatonic

3

A♭ Blues Scale

Shape One

Shape Two

A Major Pentatonic

Shape One

Shape Two

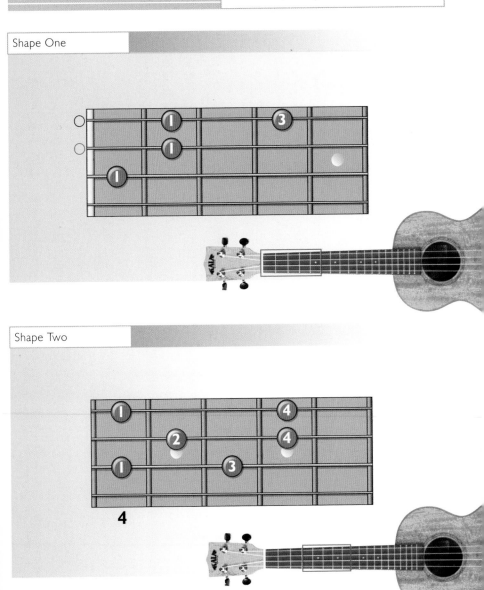

A Minor Pentatonic

Shape One

Shape Two

A Blues Scale

Shape One

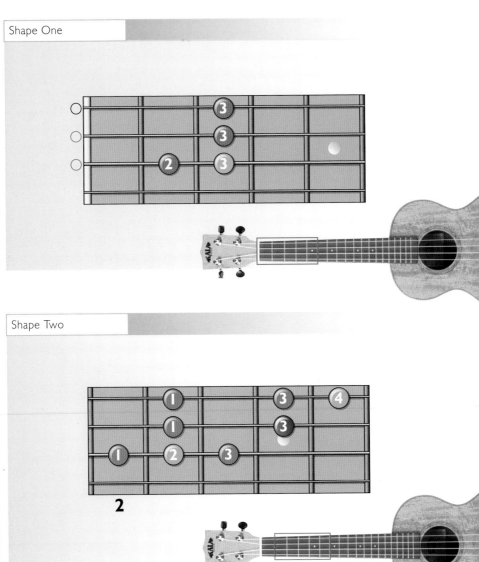

Shape Two

B♭ Major Pentatonic

Shape One

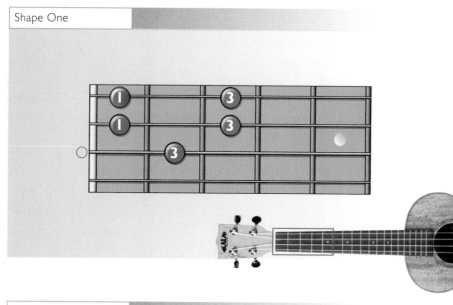

Shape Two

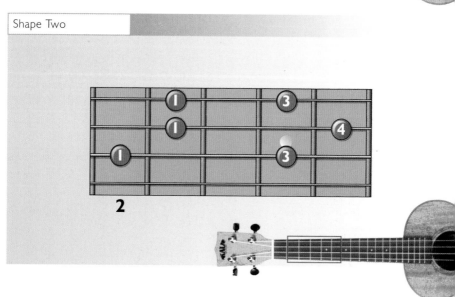

B♭ Minor Pentatonic

Shape One

Shape Two

B♭ Blues Scale

Shape One

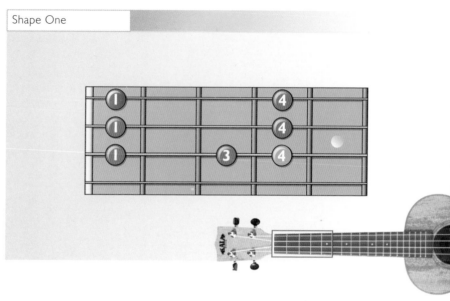

Shape Two

3

B Major Pentatonic

Shape One

Shape Two

B Minor Pentatonic

Shape One

Shape Two

B Blues Scale

Shape One

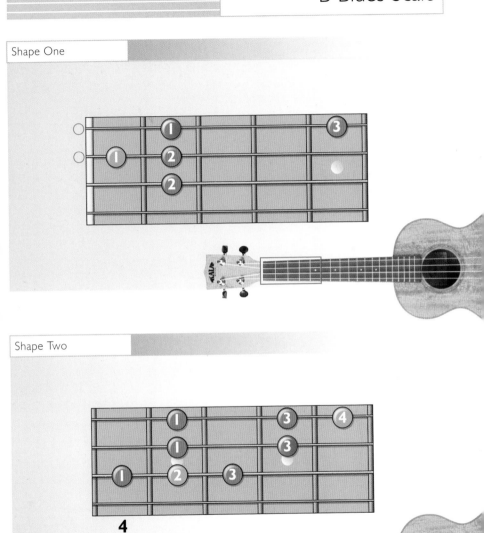

Shape Two

Chord Library

Notation Guide

Open position (first fret) chord box:

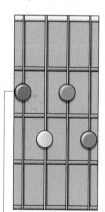

Each finger marker color coded to correspond with fretting hand fingers

Chord box beginning on third fret:

3

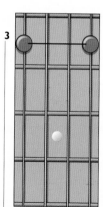

Numbers indicate where chord box starts on a higher fret

KEY

○ = open string played

●━● = barre or semibarre (color coded to indicate finger used)

CHORD ABBREVIATIONS USED

No suffix = major (i.e. C = C major), m = minor, maj7 = major 7, min7 = minor 7, 7 = dominant seventh, ° = diminished seventh

Enharmonic equivalents:
The most frequently used keys have been applied to chords with two possible names (i.e. A and G♯). If you need a chord that doesn't appear to be listed, simply look for its enharmonic equivalent, e.g. to find a Gmaj7 chord, look for F♯maj7 instead.

In this section, you'll find the shapes for every chord you'll ever need. All of the chords have been categorized by root note, not by key or type; this makes finding the shapes you need quick and easy. You'll find no "fancy" chords here, just the essential shapes you need to play in any style and in any key. Because the uke only has four strings, extended chords such as ninths, elevenths, and thirteenths often don't sound "complete." If you're playing a tune that suggests an extended chord, you can always play a seventh chord instead. Just remember to keep major chords major, minor chords minor, and dominant chords dominant. In other words, you can play Cmaj7 instead of Cmaj9, Cmin7 instead of Cmin9, and C7 instead of C9. It's all a matter of taste. Some folk like their cake with icing, others don't.

Each chord shape has its relevant CAGFD system shape indicated below it. You'll notice that not every parent chord shape will contain six parent shapes. For example, there's no "shape one" Cmin7 or C diminished chord. That's because the open strings cannot be lowered, so the shape above (i.e. shape two) has to be used instead. To find the movable version of any parent shape look at the next chord a semitone higher, i.e. the movable versions of "shape three" G chords can be found by looking at the A section. Ideally you should try to learn three shapes for every chord type (the dimensions of the uke's neck make learning all five shapes impractical). This is actually quite easy to achieve once you've learned how to play CAGFD chords in their movable forms.

C Root

C — Shape One

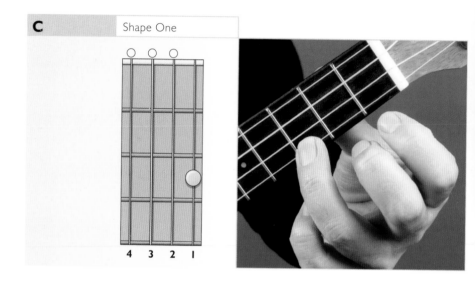

4 3 2 1

Cm — Shape One

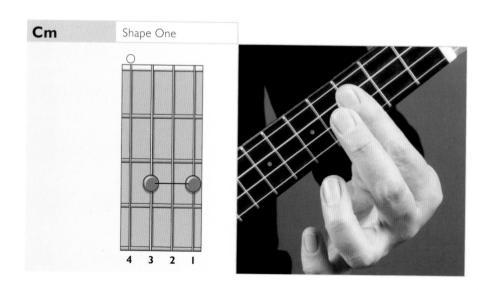

4 3 2 1

C Root

Cmaj7 | Shape One

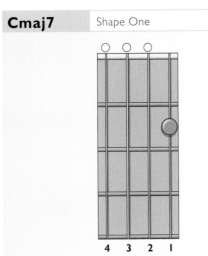

4 3 2 1

Cmin7 | Shape Two

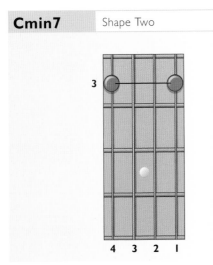

3

4 3 2 1

C Root

C7 — Shape One

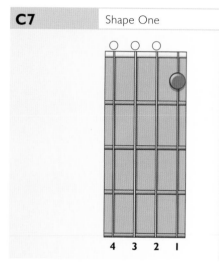

4 3 2 1

C° — Shape Two

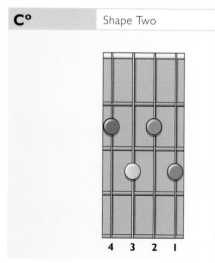

4 3 2 1

C♯ Root

C♯ — Shape One

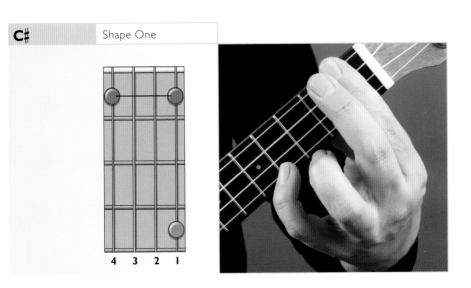

4 3 2 1

C♯m — Shape One

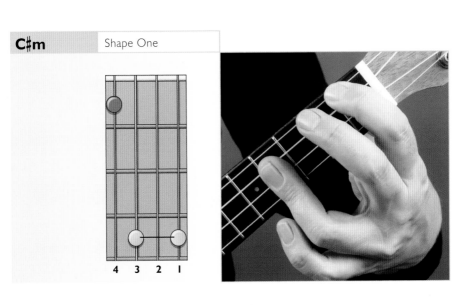

4 3 2 1

C# Root

C#maj7 Shape One

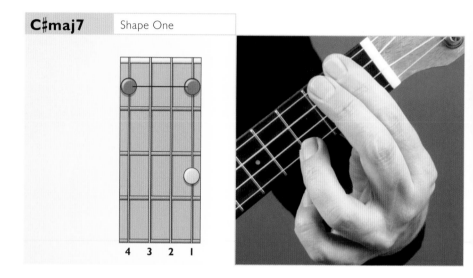

C#min7 Shape Two

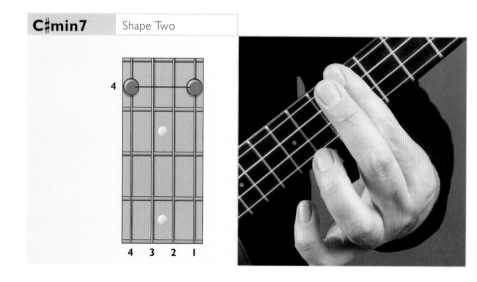

C♯ Root

C♯7

Shape One

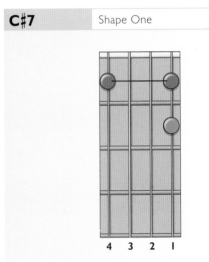

4 3 2 1

C♯°

Shape One

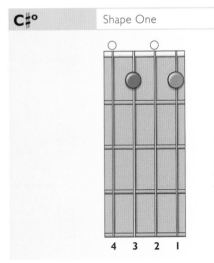

4 3 2 1

D Root

D Shape Five

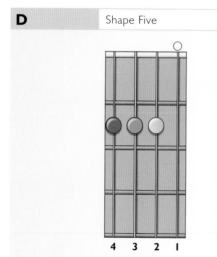

4 3 2 1

Dm Shape Five

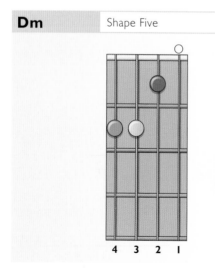

4 3 2 1

D Root

Dmaj7   Shape Five

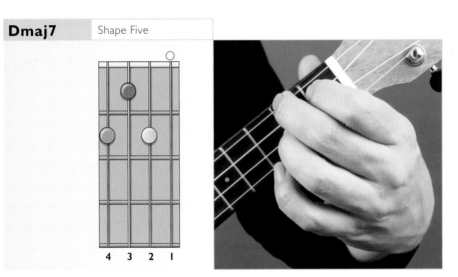

Dmin7   Shape Five

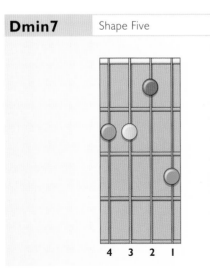

D Root

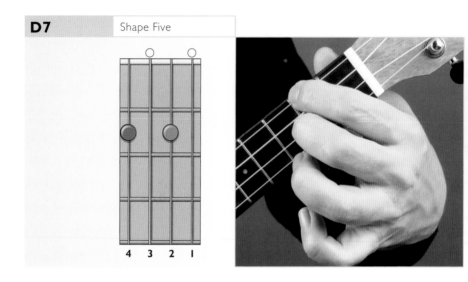

D7 Shape Five

4 3 2 1

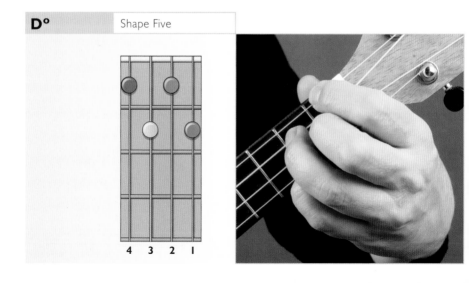

D° Shape Five

4 3 2 1

E♭ Root

E♭ — Shape Five

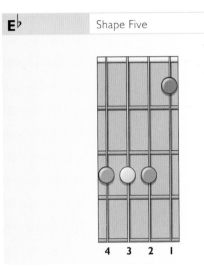

4 3 2 1

E♭m — Shape Five

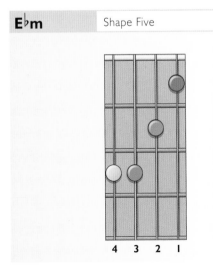

4 3 2 1

E♭ Root

E♭maj7 — Shape Five

4 3 2 1

E♭min7 — Shape Five

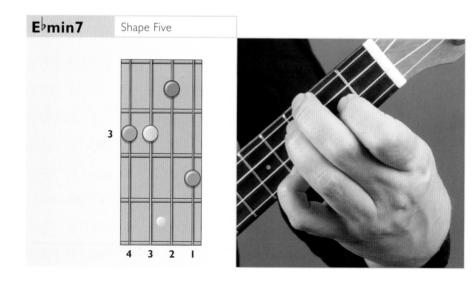

3

4 3 2 1

Eb Root

Eb7   Shape Five

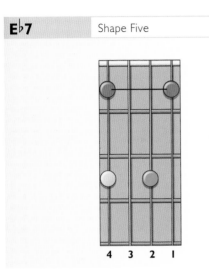

4 3 2 1

Ebo   Shape Five

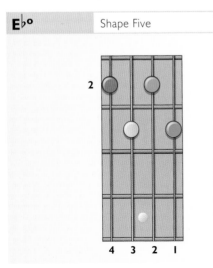

4 3 2 1

E Root

E
Shape Five

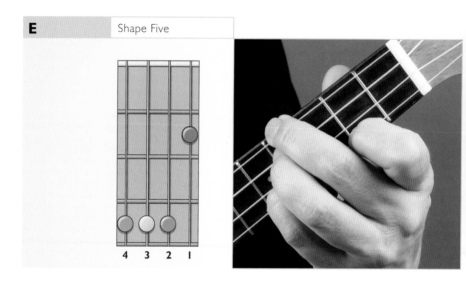

4 3 2 1

Em
Shape Five

4 3 2 1

E Root

Emaj7 Shape Four

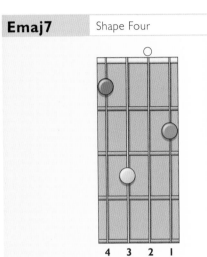

Emin7 Shape Four

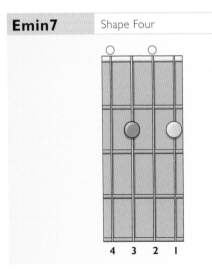

E Root

E7   Shape Four

4   3   2   I

E°   Shape Four

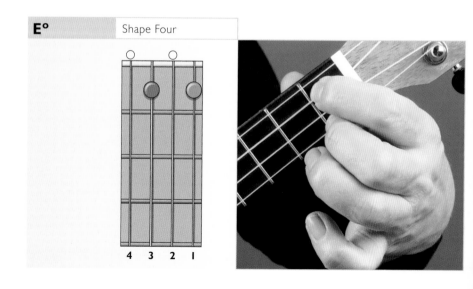

4   3   2   I

F Root

F | Shape Four

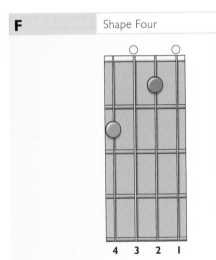

4 3 2 1

Fm | Shape Four

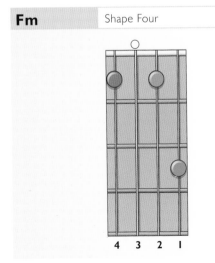

4 3 2 1

F Root

Fmaj7 | Shape Four

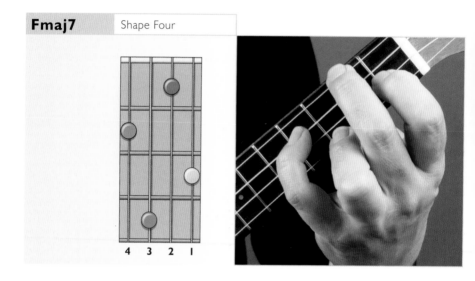

Fmin7 | Shape Four

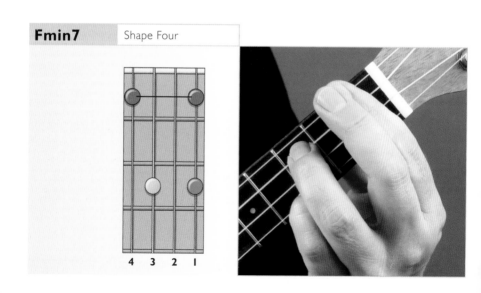

F Root

F7 — Shape Four

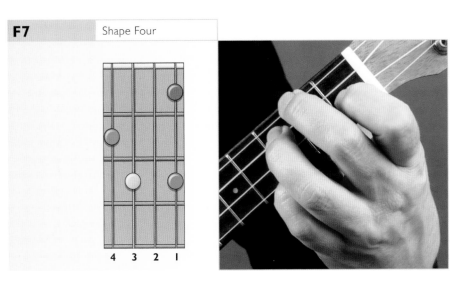

F° — Shape Four

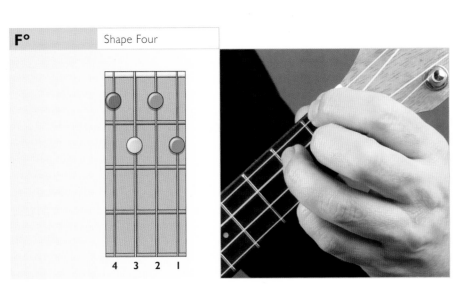

F# Root

F# Shape Four

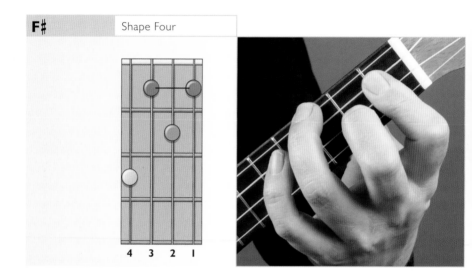

4 3 2 1

F#m Shape Four

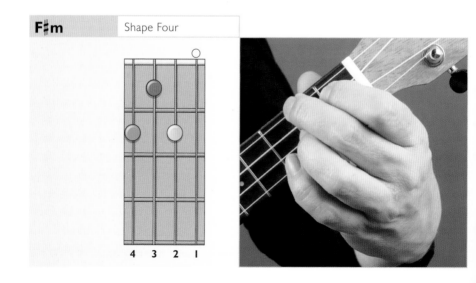

4 3 2 1

F♯ Root

F♯maj7 | Shape Four

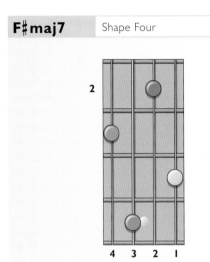

F♯min7 | Shape Four

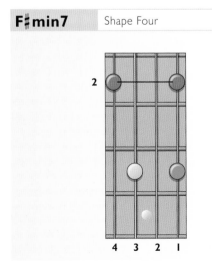

F♯ Root

F♯7 Shape Four

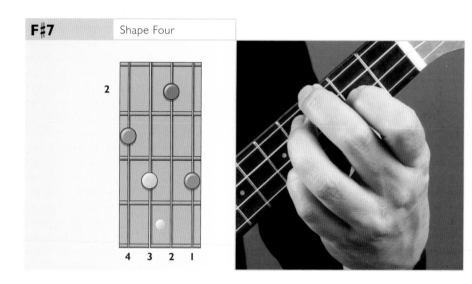

F♯° Shape Four

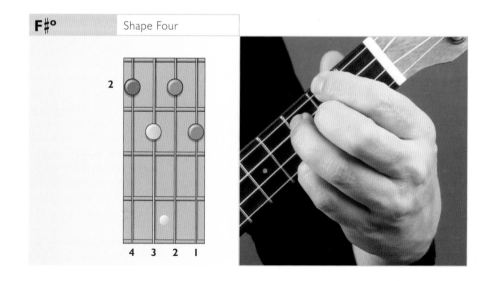

G Root

G
Shape Three

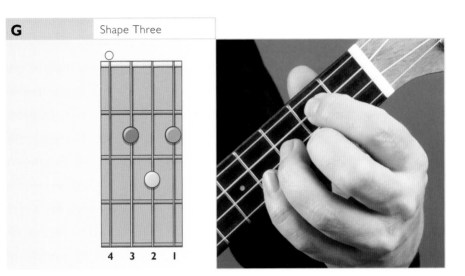

4 3 2 1

Gm
Shape Three

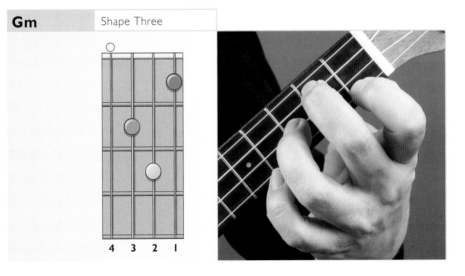

4 3 2 1

G Root

Gmaj7 | Shape Three

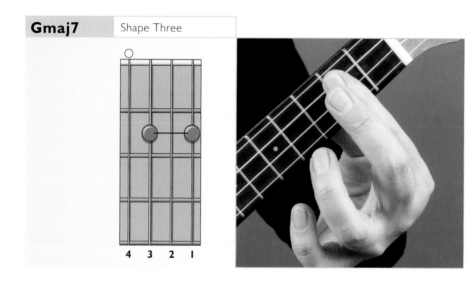

4 3 2 1

Gmin7 | Shape Three

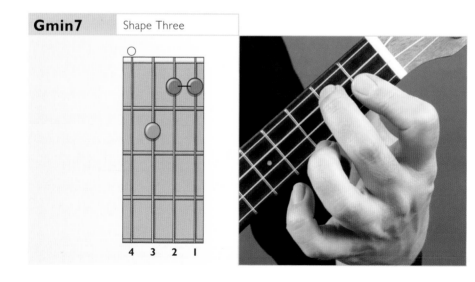

4 3 2 1

G Root

G7   Shape Three

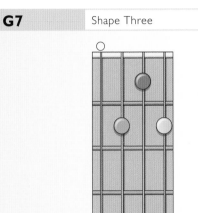

4 3 2 1

G°   Shape Three

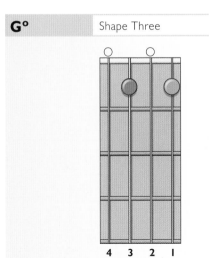

4 3 2 1

A♭ Root

A♭ — Shape Three

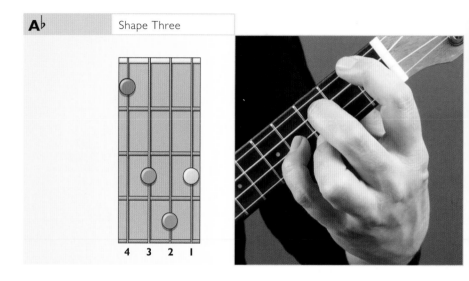

4 3 2 1

A♭m — Shape Three

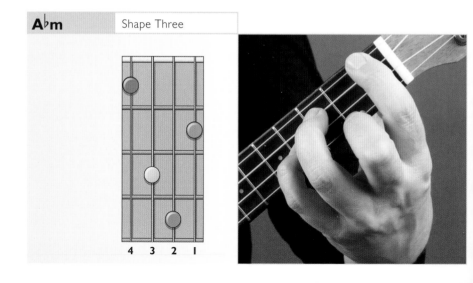

4 3 2 1

A♭ Root

A♭maj7 — Shape Three

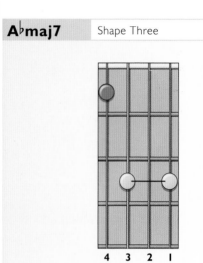

4 3 2 1

A♭min7 — Shape Three

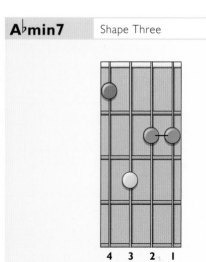

4 3 2 1

A♭ Root

A♭7   Shape Three

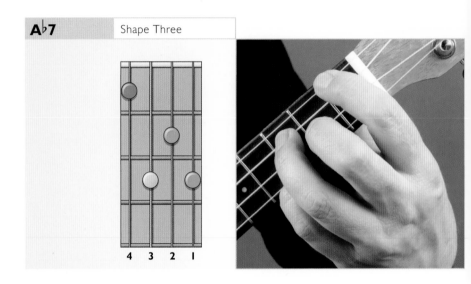

4 3 2 1

A♭°   Shape Three

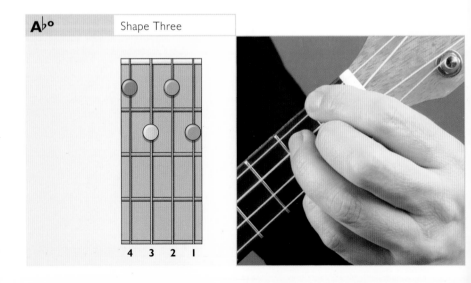

4 3 2 1

A Root

A Shape Two

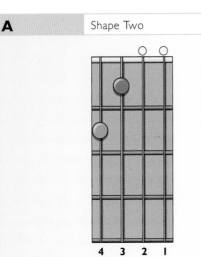

Am Shape Two

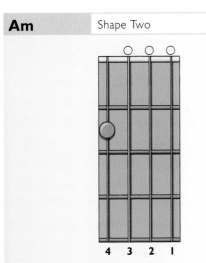

A Root

Amaj7 | Shape Two

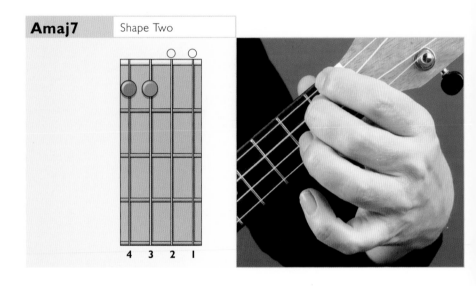

4 3 2 1

Amin7 | Shape Two

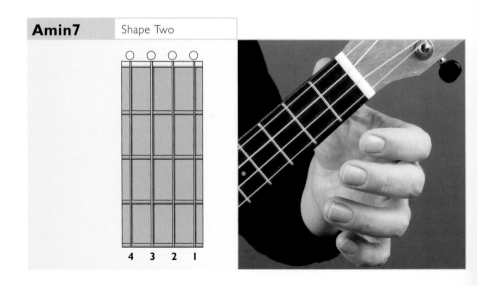

4 3 2 1

A Root

A7 — Shape Two

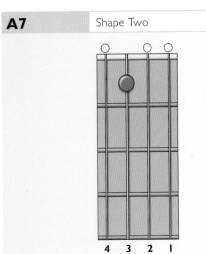

A° — Shape Three

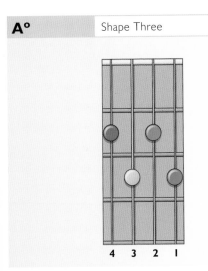

B♭ Root

B♭   Shape Two

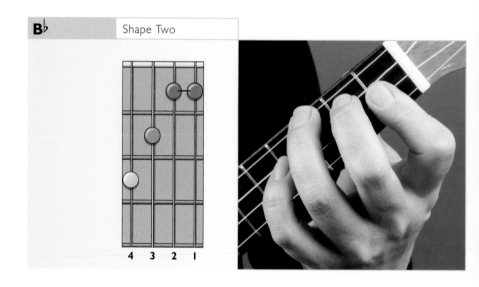

4 3 2 1

B♭m   Shape Two

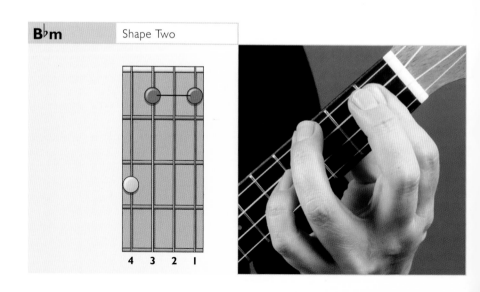

4 3 2 1

B♭ Root

B♭maj7   Shape Two

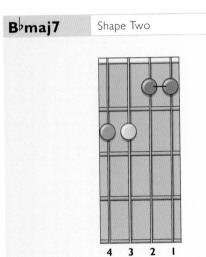

4 3 2 1

B♭min7   Shape Two

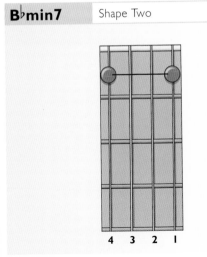

4 3 2 1

B♭ Root

B♭7 Shape Two

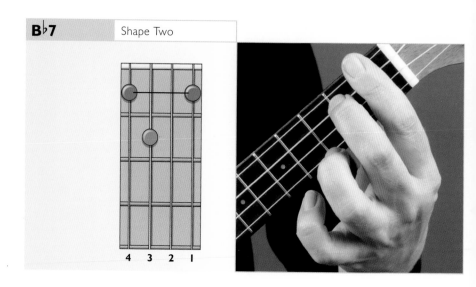

B♭° Shape Two

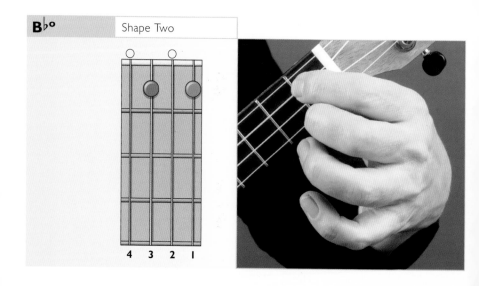

B Root

B Shape Two

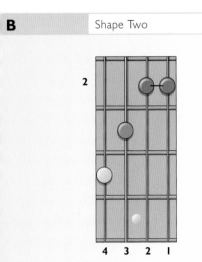

Bm Shape Two

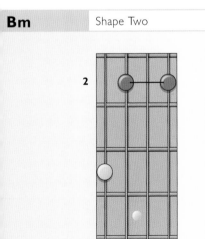

B Root

Bmaj7 | Shape Two

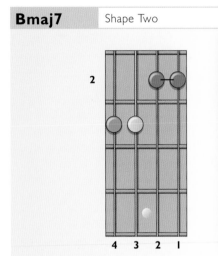

Bmin7 | Shape Two

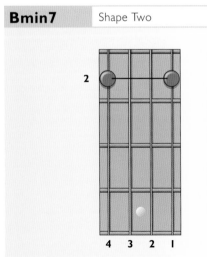

B Root

B7 — Shape Two

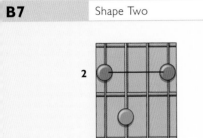

B° — Shape Two

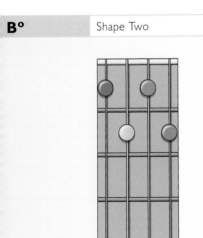

Glossary

Arpeggio: Where the notes of a chord are played melodically (i.e. without ringing into each other) as opposed to being played harmonically as in a chord. Arpeggios are invaluable tools for creating melodies and improvisations.

Backbeat: A term used to describe the emphasis of the weak beats in the bar (i.e. beats two and four in 4/4 time). The drummer usually plays the snare drum on the backbeat to create that all-important "groove."

Barre chord: By fretting across the strings with the first finger, and refingering an open chord shape in front of it, a movable chord shape can be created. The most common barre chords are shape one (based on an open E chord) and shape four (based on an open A chord).

Blue note: Traditionally, this term can be applied to any note that is "worried" by playing it slightly flat or sharp (e.g. by applying a quarter-tone bend to the minor third or minor seventh of the pentatonic scale). However, the term is also applied to the ♯4/♭5 note of the minor blues scale and the ♯2/♭3 note of the major blues scale as in this book.

Damping: Where a string(s) is muted by quickly releasing the pressure of the fretting hand, or by touching the

strings with the picking hand immediately after picking them.

Diatonic: A term applied to any note, interval, or chord that occurs naturally in a major or minor key (i.e. without requiring any scale note to be changed with a sharp, flat, or natural).

Fingerstyle: The technique of plucking the strings with the thumb and fingers, as opposed to using a pick or plectrum. It is a popular technique with country guitarists because melody and accompaniment parts can be played simultaneously.

Grace note: Distinguishable from a regular note by a smaller print size (and usually with a line through the stem) in conventional notation, or by a smaller print size number in TAB. It is used to indicate the starting note of a nonrhythmical hammer-on, pull-off, or slide, and is played quickly, just before the main note.

Hammer-on: Created by picking only the first of two ascending notes on the same string; the second note is sounded by fretting the note quickly and firmly (i.e. "hammering" the finger onto the fretboard).

Hybrid picking: A technique first developed by country guitarist Merle Travis. It involves picking a higher string

simultaneously with a note played with the plectrum. This is best achieved with your middle (*m*) or ring (*a*) picking hand fingers.

Inversion: A chord that has a note other than the root note (see Root note, opposite) as its lowest note. This is frequently the third or fifth but can also be the seventh in a seventh chord.

Legato: A term that literally means to play smoothly or "tied together." Guitarists achieve this by playing consecutive hammer-ons and pull-offs.

Let ring: An instruction usually found at the beginning of a piece of music (in brackets) or under a specific section of music (indicated by a dashed line) to indicate that notes should be allowed to continue ringing where possible (i.e. when on different strings).

Major chord: The major chord is the most consonant (i.e. stable) chord in music. It is a triad constructed from the first, third, and fifth degrees of the major scale. Often described as a "happy" sounding chord.

Minor chord: The minor chord is slightly less consonant (i.e. stable) than a major chord due to the relationship between the root and the minor third. It is constructed

from the first, third, and fifth degrees of the harmonic minor scale. Often described as a "sad" sounding chord.

Movable chord shape: A chord that does not incorporate open strings and so can be played anywhere on the neck. Movable chords are extremely useful since they allow the guitarist to play in any key. A barre chord is a movable chord shape but not all movable chord shapes are barre chords.

Offbeat: When counting in common time (4/4), the offbeats occur naturally between each beat. Counting "+" between the main beats will make it easier to locate the offbeats more accurately. A single bar of 4/4 would be counted as "1 + 2 + 3 + 4 +."

Open chord shapes: A chord played in first position (or with a capo higher up the neck) and incorporating open strings. The five principle open chord shapes are C, A, G, E, and D. Generally speaking, open chords are not movable.

Palm muting: Where the heel of the picking hand palm is gently rested on the bass strings just in front of the ukulele bridge to create muted bass notes. Used by fingerstyle players to prevent the bass notes from overpowering the melody, and rock guitarists to make the riffs sound more powerful and rhythmic.

Pickstyle: A technique involving the use of a pick (plectrum) to play the ukulele's strings.

Pinch: The process of playing two notes at the same time, achieved by picking with the thumb and a finger simultaneously.

Position: This describes the position of the left hand on the fretboard. In first position, the first finger plays notes on the first fret, the second finger notes on the second fret, etc. So, for example, in fifth position the first finger would play notes on the fifth fret, the second finger notes on the sixth fret, etc.

Pull-off: Created by picking only the first of two descending notes on the same string; the second is sounded by releasing the fretting finger with a sideways "flicking" motion.

Rubato: This literally translates from the Italian phrase *tempo rubato* as "stolen time." In other words, the musician can freely interpret the written rhythms for dramatic effect. This usually occurs in an intro or ending sequence and without accompaniment.

Riff: A repeated (ostinato) pattern, usually one or two bars in length and

often played on the lower strings of the uke.

Ritardando (abb Rit.): A gradual slowing of tempo, usually at the end of a piece of music.

Root note: The note that a chord takes its name from (i.e. the note A in an A major chord). This is usually, but not always, the lowest note of the chord.

Scale: A series of stepwise (ascending or descending) notes that follow a specific intervallic template of tones and semitones. Scales commonly consist of seven notes (i.e. the major scale), but can be fewer (i.e. the five-note pentatonic), or more (i.e. the eight-note diminished scale).

Seventh chord: A basic major, minor, or diminished triad with the seventh interval added (from the root) to create a four-note chord. From the three basic triad forms, four seventh chords can be created: major seventh, dominant seventh, minor seventh, and diminished seventh.

Slide: This is achieved by picking only the first note and then sliding the fretting finger up or down the neck without repicking. The fretting finger must maintain pressure on the fretboard when sliding or the second note will not sound.

Slur: A slur is written above or below notes on the stave (as a curved line) to indicate legato phrasing. Guitar players achieve legato phrasing with the use of hammer-ons and pull-offs.

Staccato: An instruction indicated by a dot under or above the note indicating that it should be played shorter than its written value.

Stave: The stave or staff is a system of five lines used to denote pitch in conventional music notation. Specific symbols denote the length of each note or rest (silence).

String bending: Where the pitch of a fretted note is raised by bending the string sharp with the fretting fingers. To add strength, the first and second fingers are usually added behind the third finger. String bends can be any interval from a semitone (one fret) up to a major third (four frets).

Syncopation: The emphasis of "weak" beats to create an interesting rhythm. Weak beats occur on the second and fourth beats (in 4/4 time), or on an offbeat (i.e. occurring on the "and" between the main beats).

TAB: Originally used to notate lute music during the Renaissance, this simplified form of notation indicates where a note should be played on the fretboard. It does not

indicate note duration or rests (silence).

Tone/semitone: The units used to measure the distance between notes. A tone is equivalent to a whole step (two frets), a semitone a half step (one fret).

Triad: The three notes that make up a major, minor, diminished, or augmented chord. A triad is the result of two thirds stacked on top of each other.

Index

Credits

Quarto would like to thank the following agencies and manufacturers for supplying images for inclusion in this book:

Corbis, p.45, 90
Getty Images, p.7
Press Association, p.95
Rex Features, p.11
Ukulele Orchestra of Great Britain, www.ukuleleorchestra.com, Photography: Nigel Barklie, www.pictureline.co.uk, p.74–75b

With special thanks to the Duke of Uke who supplied the ukuleles that were photographed for this book:

Duke of Uke
88 Cheshire Street
London
E2 6EH
T: +44 (0)20 358 39728
W: www.dukeofuke.co.uk

All step-by-step and other images are the copyright of Quarto Publishing plc. While every effort has been made to credit contributors, Quarto would like to apologize should there have been any omissions or errors—and would be pleased to make the appropriate correction for future editions of the book.